Gustav Kobbé

The Loves of Great Composers

Leseklassiker

Gustav Kobbé

The Loves of Great Composers

ISBN/EAN: 9783955630683

Auflage: 1

Erscheinungsjahr: 2013

Erscheinungsort: Bremen, Deutschland

@ Leseklassiker in Access Verlag GmbH, Fahrenheitstr. 1, 28359 Bremen. Alle Rechte beim Verlag und bei den jeweiligen Lizenzgebern.

Leseklassiker

The Loves of Great Composers

By Gustav Kobbé

Thomas Y. Crowell & Co.
New York

To Charles Dwyer

Table of

List of Illustrations

List of Illustrations

Mozart and His Constance

Mozart
and His Constance

EARLY eight years after Mozart's death his widow, in response to a request from a famous publishing house for relics of the composer, sent, among other Mozartiana, a packet of letters written to her by her husband. In transmitting these she wrote:

"Especially characteristic is his great love for me, which breathes through all the letters. Is it not true—those from the last year of his life are just as tender as those written during the first year of our marriage?" She added that she would like to have this fact especially mentioned "to his honor" in any biography in which the data she sent were to be used. This request was not prompted by vanity, but by a just pride in the love her husband had borne her and which she still cherished. The love of his Constance was the solace of Mozart's life.

The wonder-child, born in Salzburg in 1756, and taken by his father from court to court, where he and his sister played to admiring audiences, did not, like so many wonder-children, fade from public view, but with manhood fulfilled the promise of his early years and became one of the world's great masters of music. But his genius was not appreciated until too late. The world of to-day sees in Mozart the type of the brilliant, careless Bohemian, whom it loves to associate with art, and long since has taken him to its heart. But the world of his own day, when he asked for bread, offered him a stone.

Mozart died young; he was only thirty-five. His sufferings were crowded into a few years, but throughout these years there stood by his side one whose love soothed his trials and brightened his life,—the Constance whom he adored. What she wrote to the publishers was strictly true. His last letters to her breathed a love as fervent as the first.

Some six months before he died, she was obliged to go to Baden for her health. "You hardly will believe," he writes to her, "how heavily time hangs on my hands without you. I cannot exactly explain my feelings. There is a void that pains me; a certain longing that cannot be satisfied, hence never ceases, continues ever, aye, grows from day to day. When I think how happy and childlike we would be together in Baden and what sad, tedious hours I pass here! I take no pleasure in my work, because I cannot break it off now and then for a few words with you, as I am accustomed to. When I go to the piano and sing something from the opera ["The Magic Flute"], I have to stop right away, it affects me so. Basta! —if this very hour I could see my way clear to you, the next hour wouldn't find me here." In another letter written at this time he kisses her "in thought two thousand times."

When Mozart first met Constance, she was too young to attract his notice. He had stopped at Mannheim on his way to Paris, whither he was going with his mother on a concert tour. Requiring the services of a music copyist, he was recommended to Fridolin Weber, who eked out a livelihood by copying music and by acting as prompter at the theatre. His brother was the father of Weber, the famous composer, and his own family, which consisted of four daughters, was musical. Mozart's visit to Mannheim occurred in 1777, when Constance Weber was only fourteen.

Of her two older sisters the second, Aloysia, had a beautiful voice and no mean looks, and the young genius was greatly taken with her from the first. He induced his mother to linger in Mannheim much longer than was ne-

MOZART AT THE AGE OF ELEVEN

From a painting by Van der Smissen in the Mozarteum, Salzburg

cessary. Aloysia became his pupil; and under his tuition her voice improved wonderfully. She achieved brilliant success in public, and her father, delighted, watched with pleasure the sentimental attachment that was springing up between her and Mozart. Meanwhile Leopold Mozart was in Salzburg wondering why his wife and son were so long delaying their further journey to Paris.

When he received from Wolfgang letters full of enthusiasm over his pupil, coupled with a proposal that instead of going to Paris, he and his mother should change their destination to Italy and take the Weber family along, in order that Aloysia might further develop her talents there, he got an inkling of the true state of affairs and was furious. He had large plans for his son, knew Weber to be shiftless and the family poor, and concluded that, for their own advantage, they were endeavoring to trap Wolfgang into a matrimonial alliance. Peremptory letters sent wife and son on their way to Paris, and the elder Mozart was greatly relieved when he knew them safely beyond the confines of Mannheim.

Mozart's stay in Paris was tragically brought to an end by his mother's death. He set out for his return to Salzburg, intending, however, to stop at Mannheim, for he still remembered Aloysia affectionately. Finding that the Weber family had moved to Munich, he went there. But as soon as he came into the presence of the beautiful young singer her manner showed that her feelings toward him had cooled. Thereupon, his ardor was likewise chilled, and he continued on his way to Salzburg, where he arrived, much to his father's relief, still "unattached."

When Mozart departed from Munich, he probably thought that he was leaving behind him forever, not only the fickle Aloysia, but the rest of the

Weber family as well. How slight our premonition of fate! For, if ever the inscrutable ways of Providence brought two people together, those two were Mozart and Constance Weber. Nor was Aloysia without further influence on his career. She married an actor named Lange, with whom she went to Vienna, where she became a singer at the opera. There Mozart composed for her the rôle of Constance in his opera, "The Elopement from the Seraglio." For the eldest Weber girl, Josepha, who had a high, flexible soprano, he wrote one of his most brilliant rôles, that of the Queen of the Night in "The Magic Flute." I am anticipating somewhat in the order of events that I may correct an erroneous impression regarding Mozart's marriage, which I find frequently obtains. He composed the rôle of Constance for Aloysia shortly before he married the real Constance; and this has led many people to believe that he took the younger sister out of pique, because he had been rejected by Aloysia. Whoever believes this has a very superficial acquaintance with Mozart's biography. Five years had passed since he had parted from Aloysia at Munich. The youthful affair had blown over; and when they met again in Vienna she was Frau Lange. Mozart's marriage with Constance was a genuine love-match. It was bitterly opposed by his father, who never became wholly reconciled to the woman of his son's choice, and met with no favor from her mother. Fridolin Weber had died. Altogether the omens were unfavorable, and there were obstacles enough to have discouraged any but the most ardent couple. So much for the pique story.

Mozart went to Vienna in 1781 with the Archbishop of Salzburg, by whom, however, he was treated with such indignity that he left his service. Whom should he find in Vienna but his old friends the Webers! Frau Weber was glad enough of the opportunity to let lodgings to Mozart, for, as in Mannheim and Munich, the family was in straitened circumstances. As soon as the composer's father heard of this arrangement, he began to expostulate. Finally Mozart changed his lodgings; but this step had the very opposite effect hoped for by Leopold Mozart, for separation only increased the love that had sprung up between the young people since they had met again in Vienna, and Mozart had found the little fourteen-year-old girl of his Mannheim visit grown to young womanhood.

There seems little doubt that the Webers, with the exception of Constance, were a shiftless lot. They had drifted from place to place and had finally come to Vienna, because Aloysia had moved there with her husband. When Mozart finally decided to marry Constance, come what might, he wrote his father a letter which shows that his eyes were wide open to the faults of the family, and by the calm, almost judicial, manner in which he refers to the virtues of his future wife, that his was no hastily formed attachment, based merely on superficial attractions.

He does not spare the family in his analysis of their traits. If he seems ungallant in his references to his future Queen of the Night and to the prima donna of his "Elopement from the Seraglio," to say nothing of his former attachment for her, one must remember that this is a letter from a son to a father, in which frankness is permissible. He admits the intemperance and shrewishness of the mother; characterizes Josepha as lazy and vulgar; calls Aloysia a malicious person and a coquette; dismisses the youngest, Sophie, as too young to be anything but simply a good though thoughtless creature. Surely not an attractive picture and not a family one would enter lightly.

What drew him to Constance? Let him answer that question himself. "But the middle one, my good, dear Constance," he writes to his father, "is a martyr among them, and for that reason, perhaps, the best hearted, cleverest, and, in a word, the best among them. . . . She is neither homely nor beautiful. Her whole beauty lies in two small, dark eyes and in a fine figure. She is not brilliant, but has common sense enough to perform her duties as wife and mother. She is not extravagant; on the contrary, she is accustomed to go poorly dressed, because what little her mother can do for her children she does for the others, but never for her. It is true that she would like to be tastefully and becomingly dressed, but never expensively; and most of the things a woman needs she can make for herself. She does her own coiffure every day [head-dress must have been something appalling in those days]; understands housekeeping; has the best disposition in the world. We love each other with all our hearts. Tell me if I could ask a better wife for myself?"

The letter is so touchingly frank and simple that whoever reads it must feel that the portrait Mozart draws of his Constance is absolutely true to life. He makes no attempt to paint her as a paragon of beauty and intellect. It is a picture of the neglected member of a household—neglected because of her homely virtues, the one fair flower blooming in the dark crevice of this shiftless ménage. And at the end of the letter is the one cry which, since the world was young, has defied and brought to naught the doubting counsels of wiser heads: "We love each other with all our hearts."

The elder Mozart, fearful for his son's future, had kept himself informed of what was going on in Vienna. He knew that when his son's attentions to Constance became marked, her guardian had compelled him to sign a promise of marriage. In this the father again saw a trap laid for his son, who in worldly matters was as unversed as a child. But Leopold Mozart did not know how the episode ended, and little suspected that future generations would see in it one of the most charming incidents in the love affairs of great men. For, when her guardian had left the house, Constance asked her mother for the paper, and as soon as she had it in her hands, tore it up, exclaiming: "Dear Mozart, I do not need a written promise from you. I trust your words."

Frau Weber saw in Mozart, the suitor, a possible contributor to the household expenses, and as soon as she learned that he and Constance intended to set up for themselves, she became bitterly opposed to the match. Finally a titled lady, Baroness von Waldstädter, took the young people under her protection, and Constance went to live with her to escape her mother's nagging. Frau Weber then planned to force her daughter to return to her by legal process. Immediate marriage was the only method of escape from the scandal this would entail; and so, August 4, 1782, Mozart and his Constance were married in the Church of St. Stephen, Vienna. When at last they had all obstacles behind them and stood at the altar as one, they were so overcome by their feelings that they began to cry; and the few bystanders, including the priest, were so deeply affected by their happiness that they too were moved to tears.

Although poor, Mozart, through his music, had become acquainted with titled personages and was known at court. He and Constance, shortly after their wedding, were walking in the Prater with their pet dog. To make the dog bark, Mozart playfully pretended to strike Constance with his cane. At that moment the Emperor, chancing to come out of a summer house and seeing Mozart's action, which he mis-interpreted, began chiding him for abusing his wife so shortly after they had been married. When his mistake was explained to him, he was highly amused. Later he could not fail to hear of the couple's devotion. "Vienna was witness to these relations," wrote a contemporary of Mozart's and Con-stance's love for each other; and when Aloysia and her husband quarrelled and separated, the Emperor, meeting Constance and referring to her sister's troubles, said, "What a difference it makes to have a good husband."

In spite of poverty and its attendant struggles, Mozart's marriage was a happy one, because it was a marriage of love. Like every child of genius, he had his moods, but Constance adapted herself to them and thereby won his confidence and gained an influence over him which, however, she brought into play only when the occasion de-manded. When he was thinking out a work, he was absent-minded, and at such times she always was ready to humor him, and even cut his meat for him at table, as he was apt during such periods of abstraction to injure himself. But when he had a composition well in mind, to put it on paper seemed little more to him than copying; and then he loved to have her sit by him and tell him stories—yes, regular fairy tales and children's stories, as if he himself still were a child. He would write and listen, drop his pen and laugh, and then go on with work again. The day before the first performance of "Don Giovanni," when the final rehearsal already had been held, the overture still remained unwritten. It had to be written overnight, and it was she who sat by him and relieved the rush and strain of work with her cheerful prattle. It is said that, among other things, she read to him the story of "Aladdin and the Wonderful Lamp." Be that as it may;—she rubbed the lamp, and the overture to "Don Giovanni" appeared.

Would that their life could be portrayed in a series of such charming pictures! but grinding poverty was there also, and the bitterness of disappointed hopes. His sensitive nature could not withstand the repeated material shocks to which it was subjected. And the pity is, that it gave way just when there seemed a prospect of a change. "The Magic Flute" had been produced with great success, and that in the face of relentless opposition from envious rivals; and orders from new sources and on better terms were coming to him. But the turn of the tide was too late. When he received an order for a Requiem from a person who wished his identity to remain unknown —he was subsequently discovered to be a nobleman, who wanted to produce the work as his own—Mozart already felt the hand of death upon him and declared that he was composing the Requiem for his own obsequies. Even after he was obliged to take to his bed, he worked at it, saying it was to be his Requiem and must be ready in time. The afternoon before he died, he went over the completed portions with three friends, and at the Lachrymosa burst into tears. In the evening he lost consciousness, and early the following morning, December 5, 1791, he passed away. The immediate cause of death was rheumatic fever with typhoid complications, and his distracted widow, hoping to catch the same disease and be carried away by it, threw herself upon his bed. She was too prostrated to attend his funeral, which, be it said to the shame of his friends, was a shabby affair. The day was stormy, and after the service indoors they left before the actual burial, which was in one of the "common graves," holding ten or twelve bodies and intended to be worked over every few years for new interments. When, as soon as Con-

CONSTANCE, WIFE OF MOZART

From an engraving by Nissen

stance was strong enough, she visited the cemetery there was a new grave-digger, who upon being questioned could not locate her husband's grave, and to this day Mozart's last resting-place is unknown.

It must not be reckoned against Constance that, eighteen years after Mozart's death, she married again. For she did not forget the man on whom her heart first was set. Her second husband, Nissen, formerly Danish chargé d'affaires in Vienna, is best known by the biography of Mozart which he wrote under her guidance. They removed to Mozart's birthplace, Salzburg, where Nissen died in 1826. Constance's death was strangely associated with Mozart's memory. It was as if in her last moments she must go back to him who was her first love. For she died in Salzburg, on March 6, 1842, a few hours after the model for the Mozart monument, which adorns one of the spacious squares of the city where the composer was born, was received there. She had been the life-love of a child of genius and, without being singularly gifted herself, had understood how to humor his whims and adapt herself to his moods in which sunshine often was succeeded by shadow. It was singularly appropriate that, surviving him many years, she yet died under circumstances which formed a new link between her and his memory.

LUDWIG VAN BEETHOVEN.

After the painting by Stieler. The original in the possession of the Countess
Rosalie von Sauerma, *née* Spohr, Berlin

Beethoven
and His
"Immortal Beloved"

NE day when Baron Spaun, an old Viennese character and a friend of Beethoven's, entered the composer's lodgings, he found the man, every line of whose face denoted, above all else, strength of character, bending over a portrait of a woman and weeping, as he muttered, "You were too good, too angelic!" A moment later, he had thrust the portrait into an old chest and, with a toss of his well-set head, was his usual self again.

As Spaun was leaving, he said to the composer, "There is nothing evil in your face to-day, old fellow."

"My good angel appeared to me this morning," was Beethoven's reply.

After the composer's death, in 1827,

the portrait was found in the old chest, and also a letter, in his handwriting and evidently written to a woman, whose name, however, was not given, but who was addressed by Beethoven as his "Immortal Beloved." The letter was regarded as a great find, and biographer after biographer has stated that it must have been written to the Countess Giulietta Guicciardi, to whom he dedicated the famous "Moonlight Sonata." There was, however, one woman, who survived Beethoven more than thirty years, and who, during that weary stretch of time, knew whose was the portrait that had been found in the old chest and the identity of the woman who had returned to him the letter addressed to his "Immortal Beloved," after the strange severance of relations which both had continued to hold sacred. But she suffered in silence, and never even knew what had become of the picture.

This precious picture, which Beethoven had held in his hands and wetted with his tears, passed, with his death, into the possession of his brother Carl's widow. No one knew who it was, or took any interest in it. In 1863 a Viennese musician, Joseph Hellmesberger, succeeded in having Beethoven's remains transferred to a metallic casket, and the Beethoven family, in recognition of his efforts, made him a present of the portrait. Later it was acquired by the Beethoven Museum, in Bonn, where the master was born in 1772. There it hangs beside his own portrait, and on the back still can be read the inscription, in a feminine hand:

"To the rare genius, the great artist, and the good man, from T. B."

Who was "T. B."? If some one who had recently seen the Bonn portrait should chance to visit the National Museum in Budapest, he would come upon the bust of a woman whose features seemed familiar to him. They would grow upon him as those of the woman with the yellow shawl over her light-brown hair, a drapery of red on her shoulders and fastened at her throat, who had looked out at him from the Bonn portrait. The bust, made at a more advanced age, he would find had been placed in the museum in honor of the woman who founded the first home for friendless children in the Austrian Empire; and her name? Countess Therese Brunswick. She was Beethoven's "Immortal Beloved." "T. B."—Therese Brunswick. She was the woman who knew that the portrait found in the old chest was hers; and that the letter had been received by her shortly after her secret betrothal to Beethoven, and returned by her to him when he broke the engagement because he loved her too deeply to link her life to his.

The tragedy of their romance lay in its non-fulfilment. Beethoven was a man of noble nature, yet what had he to offer her in return for her love? His own love, it is true. But he was uncouth,

COUNTESS THERESE VON BRUNSWICK

From the portrait by Ritter von Lampir in the Beethoven-Haus at Bonn
Redrawn by Reich

stricken with deafness, and had many of the "bad moments" of genius. He foresaw unhappiness for both, and, to spare her, took upon himself the great act of renunciation. We need only recall him weeping over the picture of his Therese. And Therese? To her dying day she treasured his memory. Very few shared her secret. Her brother Franz, Beethoven's intimate friend, knew it. Baron Spaun also divined the cause of his melancholy. Some years after the composer's death, Countess Therese Brunswick conceived a great liking for a young girl, Miriam Tenger, whom she had taken under her care for a short period, until a suitable school was selected for her in Vienna. When the time for parting came, Miriam burst into tears and clung to the Countess's hand.

"Child! Child!" exclaimed the lady, "do you really love me so deeply?"

"I love you, I love you so," sobbed the child, "that I could die for you."

The Countess placed her hand on the girl's head. "My child," she said, "when you have grown older and wiser, you will understand what I mean when I say that to live for those we love shows a far greater love, because it requires so much more courage. But while you are in Vienna, there is one favor you can do me, which my heart will consider a great one. On the twenty-seventh of every March go to the Wahringer Cemetery and lay a wreath of immortelles on Beethoven's grave."

When, true to her promise, the girl went with her school principal to the cemetery, they found a man bending over the grave and placing flowers upon it. He looked up as they approached.

"The child comes at the request of the Countess Therese Brunswick," explained the principal.

"The Countess Therese Brunswick! Immortelles upon this grave are fit from her alone." The speaker was Beethoven's faithful friend, Baron Spaun.

In 1860, when the leaves of thirty-three autumns had fallen upon the composer's grave and the Countess had gone to her last resting-place, a voice, like an echo from a dead past, linked the names of Beethoven and the woman he had loved. There was at that time in Germany a virtuosa, Frau Hebenstreit, who when a young girl had been a pupil of Beethoven's friend, the violinist Schuppanzigh. At a musical, in the year mentioned, she had just taken part in a performance of the third "Leonore" overture, when, as if moved to speak by the beauty of the music, she suddenly said: "Only think of it! Just as a person sits to a painter for a portrait, Countess Therese Brunswick was the model for Beethoven's Leonore. What a debt the world owes her for it!" After a pause she went on: "Beethoven never would have dared marry without money, and a countess, too—and so refined, and delicate enough to blow away. And he—an angel and a demon in one! What would have become of them both, and of his genius with him?" So far as I have been able to discover, this was the first even semi-public linking of the two names.

Yet all these years there was one person who knew the secret—the woman who as a school-girl had placed the wreath of immortelles on Beethoven's grave for her much-loved Countess Therese Brunswick. Through this act of devotion Miriam Tenger seemed to become to the Countess a tie that stretched back to her past, and though they saw each other only at long intervals, Miriam's presence awakened anew the old memories in the Countess's heart, and from her she heard piecemeal, and with pauses of years between, the story of hers and Beethoven's romance.

Therese was the daughter of a noble house. Beethoven was welcome both as teacher and guest in the most aristocratic circles of Vienna. The noble men and women who figure in the dedications of his works were friends, not merely patrons. Despite his uncouth manners and appearance, his genius, up to the point at least when it took its highest flights in the "Ninth Symphony" and the last quartets, was appreciated; and he was a figure in Viennese society. The Brunswick house was one of many that were open to him. The Brunswicks were art lovers. Franz, the son of the house, was the composer's intimate friend. The mother had all possible graciousness and charm, but with it also a passionate pride in her family and her rank, a hauteur that would have caused her to regard an alliance between Therese and Beethoven as monstrous. Therese was an exceptional woman. She had an oval, classic face, a lovely disposition, a pure heart and a finely cultivated mind. The German painter, Peter Cornelius, said of her that any one who spoke with her felt elevated and ennobled. The family was of the right mettle. The Countess Blanka Teleki, who was condemned to death for complicity in the Hungarian uprising of 1848, but whose sentence was commuted to life imprisonment, — she finally was released in 1858, — was Therese's niece, and is said to have borne a striking likeness to her. It may be mentioned that Giulietta Guicciardi, of the "Moonlight Sonata," was Therese's cousin. There seems no doubt that the composer was attracted to Giulietta before he fell in love with his "Immortal Beloved." That is why his biographers were so ready to believe that the letter was addressed to the lady with the romantic name and identified with one of his most romantic works.

Therese herself told Miriam that one day Giulietta, who had become the affianced of Count Gallenberg, rushed into her room, threw herself at her feet like a "stage princess," and cried out:

"Counsel me, cold, wise one! I long to give Gallenberg his <u>congé</u> and marry the wonderfully ugly, beautiful Beethoven, if—if only it did not involve lowering myself socially." Therese, who worshipped the composer's genius and already loved him secretly, turned the subject off, fearful lest she should say, in her indignation at the young woman who thought she would be lowering herself by marrying Beethoven, something that might lead to an irreparable breach. "Moonlight Sonata," or no "Moonlight Sonata," there are two greater works by the same genius that bear the Brunswick name,—the "Appassionata," dedicated to Count Franz Brunswick, and the sonata in F-sharp major, Opus 78, dedicated to Therese, and far worthier of her chaste beauty and intellect than the "Moonlight."

It will be noticed that Giulietta called Therese the "cold, wise one." Her purity led her own mother to speak of her as an "anchoress." Yet it was she who from the time she was fifteen years old to the day of her death cherished the great composer in her heart; and of her love for him were the mementos that he sacredly guarded. When Therese was fifteen years old she became Beethoven's pupil. The lessons were severe. Yet beneath the rough exterior she recognized the heart of a noble man. The "cold, wise one," the "anchoress," fell in love with him soon after the lessons began, but carefully hid her feelings from every one. There is a charming anecdote of the early acquaintance of the composer and Therese.

The children of the house of Brunswick were carefully brought up. During the music lessons the mother was accustomed to sit in an adjoining room with the door between open. One bitterly cold winter day Beethoven arrived at the appointed hour. Therese had practised diligently, but the work was difficult and, in addition, she was nervous. As a result she began too fast, became disconcerted when Beethoven gruffly called out "Tempo!" and made mistake after mistake, until the master, irritated beyond endurance, rushed from the room and the house in such a hurry that he forgot his overcoat and muffler. In a moment Therese had picked up these, reached the door and was out in the street with them, when the butler overtook her, relieved her of them and hurried after the composer's retreating figure.

When the girl entered the doorway again, she came face to face with her mother, who, fortunately, had not seen her in the street, but who was scandalized that a daughter of the house of Brunswick should so far have forgotten herself and her dignity as to have run after a man even if only to the front door, and with his overcoat and muffler. "He might have caught cold and died," gasped Therese, in answer to her mother's remonstrance. What would the mother have said had she known that her daughter actually had run out into the street, and had been prevented from following Beethoven until she overtook him only by the butler's timely action!

Therese's brother Franz was devoted to her. As a boy he had taken his other sister (afterward Blanka Teleki's mother) out in a boat on the "Mediterranean," one of the ponds at Montonvasar, the Brunswick country estate. The boat upset. Therese, who was watching them from the bank, rushed in and hauled them out. Franz was asked if he had been frightened. "No," he answered, "I saw my good angel coming."

When he became intimate with Beethoven, he told the composer about this incident, and also how, after that stormy music lesson, Therese had started to overtake him with his coat and muffler. Knowing what a lonely, unhappy existence the composer led, he could not help adding that life would

be very different if he had a good angel
to watch over him, such as he had in
his sister.

Franz little knew that his words fell
upon Beethoven like seed on eager soil.
From that time on he looked at Therese with different eyes. His own love
soon taught him to know that he was
loved in return. No pledge had yet
passed between them when, in May,
1806, he went to Montonvasar on a
visit; but one evening there, when Therese was standing at the piano listening to him play, he softly intoned
Bach's—

> "Would you your true heart show me,
>   Begin it secretly,
> For all the love you trow me,
>   Let none the wiser be.
> Our love, great beyond measure,
>   To none must we impart;
> So, lock our rarest treasure
>   Securely in your heart."

Next morning they met in the park.
He told her that at last he had disco-

vered in her the model for his Leonore, the heroine of his opera "Fidelio." "And so we found each other"—these were the simple words with which, many years later, Therese concluded the narrative of her betrothal with Beethoven to Miriam Tenger.

The engagement had to be kept a secret. Had it become known, it would have ended in his immediate dismissal by the Countess' mother. In only one person was confidence reposed, Franz, the devoted brother and treasured friend. Therese's income was small, and Franz, knowing the opposition with which the proposed match would meet, pointed out to Beethoven that it would be necessary for him to secure a settled position and income before the engagement could be published and the marriage take place. The composer himself saw the justice of this, and assented.

Early in July Beethoven left Montonvasar for Furen, a health resort on the

"BEETHOVEN AT HEILIGENSTADT"

From the painting by Carl Schmidt

Plattensee, which he reached after a hard trip. Fatigued, grieving over the first parting from Therese, and downcast over his uncertain future, he there wrote the letter to his "Immortal Beloved," which is now one of the treasures of the Berlin Library. It is a long letter, much too long to be given here in full, written for the most part in ejaculatory phrases, and curiously alternating between love, despair, courage and hopefulness and commonplace, everyday affairs. Nor will space permit me to tell how Alexander W. Thayer, an American, who spent a great part of his life and means in gathering detailed and authentic data for a Beethoven biography,—which, however, he did not live to finish,—worked out the year in which this letter was written (Beethoven gave only the day of the month); showed that it must be 1806; proved further that it could not have been intended for Giulietta Guicciardi, yet did not venture to state that Countess Therese Brunswick was the undoubted recipient. Afterward, I believe, he heard of Miriam Tenger, entered into correspondence with her, and the letters doubtless will be found among his papers; but he did not live to make use of the information.

One of the reasons why the identity of the recipient of Beethoven's letter remained so long unknown was that he did not address her by name. The letter begins: "My angel, my all, myself!" In order to secure a fixed position, Beethoven had decided to try Prussia and even England, and this intention he refers to when, after apostrophizing Therese as his "immortal beloved," he writes these burning words:

"Yes, I have decided to toss abroad so long, until I can fly to your arms and call myself at home with you, and let my soul, enveloped in your love, wander through the kingdom of spirits." The letter has this exclamatory postscript:

"Eternally yours!
Eternally mine!
Eternally one another's!"

The engagement lasted until 1810, four years, when the letters, which through Franz's aid had passed between Beethoven and Therese, were returned. Therese, however, always treasured as one of her "jewels" a sprig of immortelle fastened with a ribbon to a bit of paper, the ribbon fading with passing years, the paper growing yellow, but still showing the words: "L'Immortelle à son Immortelle — Luigi."

It had been Beethoven's custom to enclose a sprig of immortelle in nearly every letter he sent her, and all these sprigs she kept in her desk many, many years. She made a white silken pillow of the flowers; and, when death came at last, she was laid at rest, her head cushioned on the mementos of the man she had loved.

Mendelssohn and His Cécile

Mendelssohn
and His Cécile

 ENDELSSOHN was a pop-
ular idol. On his death the
mournful news was plac-
arded all over Leipsic, where
he had made his home, and there was
an immense funeral procession. When
the church service was over, a woman
in deep mourning was led to the bier,
and sinking down beside it, remained
long in prayer. It was Cécile taking her
last farewell of Felix.

Mendelssohn was born under a lucky
star. The pathways of most musical
geniuses are covered with thorns; his
was strewn with roses. The Mendelssohn family, originally Jewish, was
well-to-do and highly refined, and Felix's grandfather was a philosophical
writer of some note. This inspired the
oft-quoted mot of the musician's father: "Once I was known as the son

of the famous Mendelssohn; now I am known as the father of the famous Mendelssohn."

Felix was an amazingly clever, fascinating boy. Coincident with his musical gifts he had a talent for art. Goethe was captivated by him, and the many distinguished friends of the Mendelssohn house in Berlin adored him. This house was a gathering place of artists, musicians, literary men and scientists; his genius had the stimulus found in the "atmosphere" of such a household. There was one member of that household between whom and himself the most tender relations existed, — his sister Fanny, who became the wife of Hensel, the artist. The musical tastes of Felix and Fanny were alike: she was the confidante of his ambitions, and thus was created between them an artistic sympathy, which from childhood greatly strengthened the family bond. Growing up amid love and devotion, to say nothing of the admira-

FÉLIX MENDELSSOHN-BARTHOLDY

tion accorded his genius in the home circle, with tastes, naturally refined, cultivated to the utmost both by education and absorption, he was apt to be most fastidious in the choice of a wife. Fastidiousness in everything was, in fact, one of his traits. One has but to recall how, one after another, he rejected the subjects that were offered him for operatic composition. "I am afraid," said his father, who was quite anxious to see his famous son properly settled in life, "that Felix's censoriousness will prevent his getting a wife as well as a libretto."

It may have been a regretful feeling that he had disappointed his father by not marrying which led him, after the latter's sudden death in November, 1835, to consider the matter more seriously. He hastened to Berlin to his mother, and then returned to Leipsic, where he had charge of the famous Gewandhaus concerts. He settled down to work again, and especially to finish his oratorio of "St. Paul." In March, 1836, the University of Leipsic made him a Ph.D.

In May or June of this year a friend and colleague named Schelble, who conducted the Cæcilia Singing Society at Frankfort-on-the-Main, was taken ill, and, desiring to rest and recuperate, asked Mendelssohn to officiate in his place. The request came at an inconvenient time, for he had planned to take some recreation himself, and had mapped out a tour to Switzerland and Genoa. But Felix was an obliging fellow, and promptly responded with an affirmative when his colleague called upon him for aid. The unselfish relinquishment of his intended tour was to meet with a further reward than that which comes from the satisfaction of a good deed done at some self-sacrifice, and this reward was the more grateful because unexpected by his friends, his family, or even himself. Yet it was destined to delight them all.

Felix was in Frankfort six weeks. So short a period rarely leads to a decisive event in a man's life, but did so in Mendelssohn's case. He occupied lodgings in a house on the Schöne Aussicht (Beautiful View), with an outlook upon the river. But there was another beautiful view in Frankfort which occupied his attention far more, for among those he met during his sojourn in the city on the Main was Cécile,—Cécile Charlotte Sophie Jeanrenaud. Her father, long dead, had been the pastor of the French Walloon Reformed Church in Frankfort, where his widow and children moved in the best social circles of the city. Cécile, then seventeen (ten years younger than Felix), was a "beauty" of a most delicate type. Mme. Jeanrenaud still was a fine-looking woman, and possibly because of this fact, coupled with Felix's shy manner in the presence of Cécile, now that for the first time his heart was deeply touched, it was at first supposed that he was courting the mother; and her children, Cécile included, twitted her on it.

Now Felix acted in a manner characteristic of his bringing up and of the bent of his genius. Mozart, Beethoven, Chopin, Schumann, Liszt, Wagner—not one of these hesitated a moment where his heart was concerned. If anything, they were too impetuous. They are the masters of the passionate expression in music; Mendelssohn's music is of the refined, delicate type—like his own bringing up. The perfectly polished "Songs without Words," the smoothly flowing symphonies, the lyric violin concerto—these are most typical of his genius. Only here and there in his works are there fitful flashes of deeper significance, as in certain dramatic passages of the "Elijah" oratorio. And so, when Felix found himself possessed of a passion for Cécile Jeanrenaud, the beautiful, he did not throw himself at her feet and pour out a confession of love to her. Far from it. With a calmness that would make one feel like pinching him, were it not that after all the story has a "happy ending," he left Frankfort at the end of six weeks, when his feelings were at their height, and in order to submit the state of his affections to a cool and unprejudiced scrutiny, he went to Scheveningen, Holland, where he spent a month. Anything more characteristically Mendelssohnian can scarcely be imagined than this leisurely passing of judgment on his own heart.

Just what Cécile thought of his sudden departure we do not know. No doubt by that time she had ceased twitting her mother on Felix's supposed intentions to make Frau Mendelssohn of Mme. Jeanrenaud, for it must have become apparent that the attentions of the famous composer were not directed toward the beautiful mother, but toward the more beautiful daughter. If, however, she felt at all uneasy at his going away at the time when he should have been preparing to declare himself, her doubts would have been dispelled could she have read some of the letters which he dispatched from Scheveningen. That she herself was captivated by him there seems no doubt. It was an amusing change from her preconceived notion of him. She had imagined him a stiff, disagreeable, jealous old man, who wore a green velvet skull-cap and played tedious fugues. This prejudice, needless to say, was dispelled at their first meeting, when she found the crabbed creation of her fancy a man of the world, with gracious, winning manners, and a brilliant conversationalist not only on music, but also on other topics.

It is a curious coincidence that when Felix left Frankfort for Scheveningen, with the image of this fair being in his heart, the Cæcilia Society should have presented him with a handsome dressing-case marked "F. M.-B. and Cæ-

FANNY HENSEL, SISTER OF MENDELSSOHN

cilia."[1] He had come to Frankfort to conduct the Cæcilia; he had met Cæcilia; and now he was at the last moment reminded that he was leaving Cæcilia behind; yet he was carrying Cæcilia with him. If there is anything prophetic in coincidences, everything pointed to the fact that Cæcilia was to play a more prominent part in his life than that of a mere name.

Even before Felix left Frankfort there were some who were in his secret. Evidently the Mendelssohn family had received reports of his attentions to the fair Cécile Jeanrenaud and were all a-flutter with happy anticipation. For there is a letter from Felix to his sister Rebecca which must have been written in answer to one from her containing something in the nature of an inquiry regarding the state of his feelings. "The present period in my life,"

[1] The "-B" on the dressing-case stands for "-Bartholdy." When the Mendelssohn family changed from Judaism to Protestantism, it added the mother's family name.

he writes to her, "is a very strange one, for I am more desperately in love than I ever was before, and I do not know what to do. I leave Frankfort the day after to-morrow, but I feel as if it would cost me my life. At all events I intend to return here and see this charming girl once more before I go back to Leipsic. But I have not an idea whether she likes me or not, and I do not know what to do to make her like me, as I already have said. But one thing is certain—that to her I owe the first real happiness I have had this year, and now I feel fresh and hopeful again for the first time. When away from her, though, I always am sad—now, you see, I have let you into a secret which nobody else knows anything about; but in order that you may set the whole world an example in discretion, I will tell you nothing more about it." He adds that he is going to detest the seashore, and ends with the exclamation, "O Rebecca! What shall I do?" Rebecca might have answered, "Tell Cécile, instead of me;" and, indeed, I wonder if she did not take occasion to drop a few hints to Cécile during her brother's absence in Holland.

There was another who might have told Cécile how Felix felt toward her, —his mother. For to her he wrote from Scheveningen that he gladly would send Holland, its dykes, sea baths, bathing-machines, Kursaals and visitors to the end of the world to be back in Frankfort. "When I have seen this charming girl again, I hope the suspense soon will be over and I shall know whether we are to be anything —or rather everything—to each other, or not." Evidently his scrutiny of his own feelings was leading him to a very definite conclusion. He was in Scheveningen, but his heart was in the city on the Main, and he was wishing himself back in the Schöne Aussicht— longing for that "beautiful view" once more.

Back to Frankfort he hied himself as soon as the month in Holland was happily over. It was not only back to Frankfort, it was back to Cécile, in every sense of the words; for if Rebecca and his mother had not conveyed to the delicate beauty some suggestion of the feelings she had inspired in Felix's heart, she herself must have become aware of them, and of something very much like in her own, since matters were not long in coming to a point after his return. He spent August at Scheveningen; in September his suspense was over, for his engagement to Cécile formally took place at Kronberg, near Frankfort. Three weeks later he was obliged to go back to his duties at Leipsic. How much he was beloved by the public appears from the fact that at the next Gewandhaus concert the directors placed on the programme, "Wer ein Holdes Weib Errungen" (He who a Lovely Wife has Won) from "Fidelio," and that when the number was

CÉCILE, WIFE OF MENDELSSOHN

reached, and Felix raised his bâton, the audience burst into applause which continued a long time. It was their congratulations to their idol on his betrothal.

"Les Feliciens" was the title given to Felix and Cécile by his sister Fanny later in life. At this time Mendelssohn himself was indescribably happy. At least, he could not himself find words in which to express all he felt. It is pleasant to find that a great composer is no exception to the rule which makes lovers "too happy for words." "But what words am I to use in describing my happiness?" he writes to his sister. "I do not know and am dumb, but not for the same reason as the monkeys on the Orinoco—far from it."

We gain an idea of Cécile's social position from Felix's statement, contained in this same letter, that he and his fiancée are obliged to make one hundred and sixty-three calls in Frankfort. This was written before he had returned to his duties in Leipsic. Christmas again found him with his betrothed and again writing to Fanny—this time about a portrait of Cécile, which her family had given him. "They gave me a portrait of her on Christmas, but it only stirred up afresh my wrath against all bad artists. She looks like an ordinary young woman flattered." (Rather a good bit of criticism.) "It really is too bad that with such a sitter the fellow could not have shown a spark of poetry." It is quite evident that Felix was much in love with his fair fiancée.

He and Cécile were married in her father's former church in March, 1837. During their honeymoon Felix wrote to his friend, Eduard Devrient, the famous actor, from the Bavarian highlands. A rare spirit of peace and contentment breathes through the letter. "You know that I am here with my wife, my dear Cécile, and that it is our wedding tour; that we already are an old married couple of six weeks' standing. There is so much to tell you that I know not how to make a beginning. Picture it to yourself. I can only say that I am too happy, too glad; and yet not at all beside myself, as I should have expected to be, but calm and accustomed, as though it could not be otherwise. But you should know my Cécile!" Evidently such a love as was here described was not a mere sentimental flash in the pan. It was an affection founded on reciprocal tastes and sympathies, the kind that usually lasts. Cécile was refined and delicate, and beautiful. She was just the woman to grace the home that a fastidious man like Mendelssohn would want to establish.

The most insistent note to be observed in his correspondence from this time on is that of a desire to remain within his own four walls. Fanny had been advised to go to the seashore for her health, but had delayed doing so because loath to leave her husband.

"Think of me," writes Felix, urging her to go, "who must in a few weeks, though we have not been married four months yet, leave Cécile here and go to England by myself—all, too, for the sake of a music festival. Gracious me! All this is no joke. But possibly the death of the King of England will intervene and put a stop to the whole project." The life of a king meant little to Felix in the distressing prospect of being obliged to leave his Cécile. Felix, the husband, was not as eager to travel as Felix, the bachelor, had been.

There are various "appreciations" of Cécile. The least enthusiastic, perhaps, is that of Hensel, Felix's brother-in-law. He says that she was not a striking person in any way, neither extraordinarily clever, brilliantly witty, nor exceptionally accomplished. But to this somewhat indefinite observation he adds that she exerted an influence as soothing as that of the open sky, or running water. Indeed, Hensel's

first frigid reserve yielded to the opinion that Cécile's gentleness and bright-
ness made Felix's life one continued
course of happiness to the end. It was
some time after the marriage before
Mendelssohn's sisters saw Cécile for
the first time. The good they heard of
her made them the more impatient to
meet her. "I tell you candidly," the
clever Fanny writes to her, "that by
this time, when anybody comes to talk
to me about your beauty and your eyes,
it makes me quite cross. I have had
enough of hearsay, and beautiful eyes
were not made to be heard." When at
last Fanny did see Cécile, this fond
sister of Felix's, who naturally would
be most critical, was enthusiastic over
her. "She is amiable, simple, fresh,
happy and even-tempered, and I consider Felix most fortunate. For though
loving him inexpressibly, she does not
spoil him, but when he is moody, meets
him with a self-restraint which in due
course of time will cure him of his mood-

iness altogether. The effect of her presence is like that of a fresh breeze, she is so light and bright and natural."

To my mind, however, Devrient has drawn the best word portrait of her. After their first meeting he wrote: "How often we had pictured the kind of woman that would be a true second half to Felix; and now the lovely, gentle being was before us, whose glance and smile alone promised all that we could desire for the happiness of our spoilt favorite." Later, Devrient finished the picture: "Cécile was one of those sweet, womanly natures whose gentle simplicity, whose mere presence, soothed and pleased. She was slender, with strikingly beautiful and delicate features; her hair was between brown and gold; but the transcendent lustre of her great blue eyes, and the brilliant roses on her cheeks, were sad harbingers of early death. She spoke little and never with animation, and in a low, soft voice. Shakespeare's words, 'my gracious si-

THE MENDELSSOHN MONUMENT IN LEIPSIG

lence,' applied to her, no less than to Cordelia."

Thus, while Cécile does not seem to have been an extraordinarily gifted woman from an artistic or intellectual point of view, it is quite evident that she possessed a refinement that must have appealed forcibly to a man brought up in such genteel surroundings and as sensitive as Mendelssohn. Such a woman must have been, after all, better suited to his delicate genius than a wife of unusual gifts would have been. For it is a helpmeet, not another genius, that a man of genius really needs most. The woman who, without being prosy or commonplace and without allowing herself to retrograde in looks or in personal care, can run a household in a systematic, orderly fashion is the greatest blessing that Providence can bestow upon genius. Evidently Cécile was just such a woman. Her tact seems to have been as delicate as her beauty. Without, perhaps, having directly inspired any composition of her husband's, her gentleness, her simple grace, doubtless left their mark on many bars of his music.

It seems doubly cruel that death should have cut Felix down when he had enjoyed but ten happy years with his Cécile. Yet had his life been long, the pang of separation would soon have come to him. Devrient had not been mistaken when he spoke of "those sad harbingers of early death;" and Cécile survived Felix scarcely five years.

Felix's death occurred at Leipsic in 1847. In September, while listening to his own recently composed "Nacht Lied" he swooned away. His system, weakened by overwork, succumbed, nervous prostration followed, and on November 4 he died. Sudden death had carried off his grandfather, father, mother and favorite sister; and he had a presentiment that his end would come about in the same way. During the dull half-sleep preceding death he spoke but once, and then to Cécile in answer to her inquiry how he felt—"Tired, very tired."

Devrient tells how he went to the house of mutual friends in Dresden for news of Mendelssohn's condition, when Clara Schumann came in, a letter in her hand and weeping, and told them that Felix had died the previous evening. Devrient hastened to Leipsic, and Cécile sent for him. I cannot close this article more fittingly than with his description of their meeting in the presence of the illustrious dead—the cherished friend of one, the husband of the other.

"She received me with the tenderness of a sister, wept in silence, and was calm and composed as ever. She thanked me for all the love and devotion I had shown to her Felix, grieved for me that I should have to mourn so faithful a friend, and spoke of the love with which Felix always had regarded me. Long we spoke of him; it comforted her, and she was loath for me to depart. She was most unpretentious in her sorrow, gentle, and resigned to live for the care and education of her children. She said God would help her, and surely her boys would have the inheritance of some of their father's genius. There could not be a more worthy memory of him than the well-balanced, strong and tender heart of this mourning widow."

Chopin
and the Countess Delphine Potocka

Chopin
and the
Countess Delphine Potocka

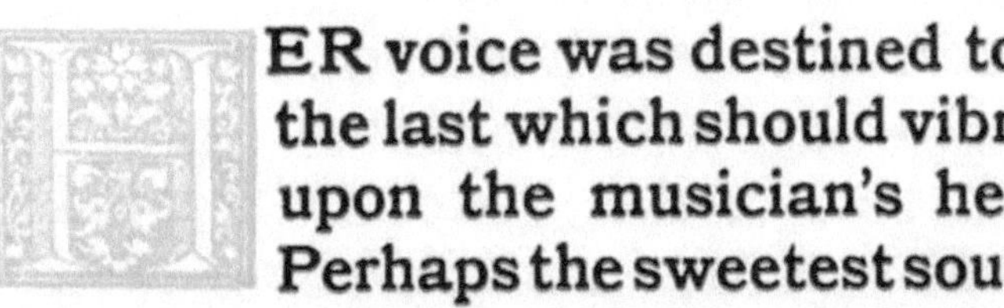

ER voice was destined to be the last which should vibrate upon the musician's heart. Perhaps the sweetest sounds of earth accompanied the parting soul until they blended in his ear with the first chords of the angels' lyres."

It is thus Liszt describes the voice of Countess Delphine Potocka as it vibrated through the room in which Chopin lay dying. Witnesses disagree regarding details. One of the small company that gathered about his bed says she sang but once, others that she sang twice; and even these vary when they name the compositions. Yet however they may differ on these minor points, they agree as to the main incident. That the beautiful Delphine sang for the dying Chopin is not a mere pleasing tradition; it is a fact. Her voice ravished the ear of the great composer, whose life was ebbing away, and soothed his last hours.

"Therefore, then, has God so long delayed to call me to Him. He wanted to vouchsafe me the joy of seeing you." These were the words Chopin whispered when he opened his eyes and saw, beside his sister Louise, the Countess Delphine Potocka, who had hurried from a distance as soon as she was notified that his end was drawing near. She was one of those rare and radiant souls who could bestow upon this delicate child of genius her tenderest friendship, perhaps even her love, yet keep herself unsullied and an object of adoration as much for her purity as for her beauty. Because she was Chopin's friend, because she came to him in his dying hours, because along paths unseen by those about them her voice threaded its way to his very soul, no

FRÉDÉRIC CHOPIN

From the portrait by Schick

life of him is complete without mention of her, and in the mind of the musical public her name is irrevocably associated with his. Each succeeding biographer of the great composer has sought to tell us a little more about her—yet little is known of her even now beyond the fact that she was very beautiful—and so eager have we been for a glimpse of her face that we have accepted without reserve as an authentic presentment of her features the famous portrait of a Countess Potocka who, I find, died some seven or eight years before Delphine and Chopin met.

But we have portraits of Delphine by Chopin himself, not drawn with pencil or crayon, or painted with brush, but her face as his soul saw it and transformed it into music. Listen to a great virtuoso play his two concertos. Ask yourself which of the six movements is the most beautiful. Surely your choice will fall on the slow movement of the second—dedicated to the Countess

Delphine Potocka, and one of the composer's most tender and exquisite productions; or play over the waltzes—the one over which for grace and poetic sentiment you will linger longest will be the sixth, dedicated to the Countess Delphine Potocka.

Liszt, who knew Chopin, tells us that the composer evinced a decided preference for the Adagio of the second concerto and liked to repeat it frequently. He speaks of the Adagio, this musical portrait of Delphine, as almost ideally perfect; now radiant with light, now full of tender pathos; a happy vale of Tempe, a magnificent landscape flooded with summer glow and lustre, yet forming a background for the rehearsal of some dire scene of mortal anguish, a contrast sustained by a fusion of tones, a softening of gloomy hues, which, while saddening joy, soothes the bitterness of sorrow.

What a lifelike portrait Chopin drew in this "beautiful, deep-toned, love-laden cantilena"! For was it not the incomparable Delphine who was destined to "soothe the bitterness of sorrow" during his final hours on earth?

But while hers was a soul strung with chords that vibrated to the slightest breath of sorrow, she could be vivacious as well. She was a child of Poland, that land of sorrow, but where sorrow, for very excess of itself, sometimes reverts to joy. And so she had her brilliant, joyous moments. Chopin saw her in such moments, too, and, that the recollection might not pass away, for all time fixed her picture in her vivacious moods in the last movement, the Allegro vivace of the concerto, with what Niecks, one of the leading modern biographers of the composer, calls its feminine softness and rounded contours, its graceful, gyrating, dance-like motions, its sprightliness and frolicsomeness. In the same way in the waltz, there is an obvious mingling of the gay and the sad, the tender and the debonair. Chopin thought he was writing a waltz. He really was writing "Delphine Po- tocka." He, too, was from Poland, and that circumstance of itself drew them to each other from the time when they first met in France.

One of Chopin's favorite musical a- musements, when he was a guest at the houses of his favorite friends, was to play on the piano musical portraits of the company. At the salon of the Countess Komar, Delphine's mother, he played one evening the portraits of the two daughters of the house. When it came to Delphine's he gently drew her light shawl from her shoulders, spread it over the keyboard, and then played through it, his fingers, with every tone they produced, coming in touch with the gossamer-like fabric, still warm and hallowed for him from its contact with her.

It seems to have been about 1830 that Delphine first came into the compos- er's life. In that year the Count and

Countess Komar and their three beautiful daughters arrived in Nice. Count Komar was business manager for one of the Potockas. The girls made brilliant matches. Marie became the Princess de Beauvau-Craon; Delphine became the Countess Potocka, and Nathalie, the Marchioness Medici Spada. The last named died a victim to her zeal as nurse during a cholera plague in Rome.

Chopin was a man who attracted women. His delicate physique, — he died of consumption, — his refined, poetic temperament, and his exquisite art as a composer combined with his beautiful piano playing, so well suited to the intimate circle of the drawing-room, to make his personality a thoroughly fascinating one. Moreover, he was, besides an artist, a gentleman, with the reserve yet charm of manner that characterizes the man of breeding. In men women admire two extremes, — splendid physical strength, or the delicacy that suggests a poetic soul. Chopin was a creator of poetic music and a gentle virtuoso. His appearance harmonized with his genius. He was one of his own nocturnes in which you can feel a vague presentiment of untimely death.

He is described as a model son, an affectionate brother and a faithful friend. His eyes were brown; his hair was chestnut, luxuriant and as soft as silk. His complexion was of transparent delicacy; his voice subdued and musical. He moved with grace. Born near Warsaw, in 1809, he was brought up in his father's school with the sons of aristocrats. He had the manners of an aristocrat, and was careful in his dress.

But despite his sensitive nature, he could resent undue familiarity or rudeness, yet in a refined way all his own. Once when he was a guest at dinner at a rich man's house in Paris, he was asked by the host to play—a patent violation of etiquette toward a distinguished artist. Chopin demurred. The host continued to press him, urging that Liszt and Thalberg had played in his house after dinner.

"But," protested Chopin, "I have eaten so little!" and thus put an end to the matter.

Some twenty or thirty of the best salons in Paris were open to him. Among them were those of the Polish exiles, some of whom he had known since their school-days at his father's. He was in the truest sense of the word a friend of those who entertained him—in fact, one of them. For a list of those among whom he moved socially read the dedications on his music. They include wealthy women, like Mme. Nathaniel de Rothschild, but also a long line of princesses and countesses. In the salon of the Potocka he was intimately at home, and it was especially there he drew his musical portraits at the piano. Delphine, his brilliant countrywoman, vibrated with music herself. She possessed "une belle voix de soprano," and sang "d'après la méthode des maîtres d'Italie."

In her salon were heard such singers as Rubini, Lablache, Tamburini, Malibran, Grisi and Persiani. Yet it was her voice Chopin wished to hear when he lay dying! Truly hers must have been a marvellous gift of song! At her salon it was his delight to accompany her with his highly poetical playing. From what is known of his delicate art as a pianist it is possible to imagine how exquisitely his accompaniments must have both sustained and mingled with that "belle voix de soprano." He had a knack of improvising a melody to any poem that happened to take his fancy, and thus he and Delphine would treat to an improvised song the élite of the musical, artistic, literary and social world that gathered in her salon. It is unfortunate that these improvisations were lightly forgotten by the composer, for he has left us few songs. Delphine "took as much trouble in giving choice

From the famous pastel in the Royal Berlin Gallery.   Artist unknown

musical entertainments as other people did in giving choice dinners." Her salon must have been a resort after the composer's own heart.

Liszt, who knew Delphine well during Chopin's lifetime, and from whose letters, as yet untranslated into English, I have been able to unearth a few references to her (the last in May, 1861, nearly twelve years after Chopin died, and the last definite reference to her which I have been able to discover), says that her indescribable and spirited grace made her one of the most admired sovereigns of the society of Paris. He speaks of her "ethereal beauty" and her "enchanting voice" which enchained Chopin. Delphine was, in fact, "famous for her rare beauty and fascinating singing."

No biography of Chopin contains so much as the scrap of a letter either from him to her, or from her to him. That he should not have written is hardly to be wondered at, considering that letter writing was most repugnant to him. He would take a long walk in order to accept or decline an invitation in person, rather than indite a brief note. Moreover, in addition to this trait, he was so often in the salon of the Countess Potocka that much correspondence with her was unnecessary. I have, however, discovered two letters from her to the composer. One, written in French, asks him to occupy a seat in her box at a Berlioz concert. The other is in Polish and is quite long. It is undated, and there is nothing to show from where it was written. Evidently, however, she had heard that he was ailing, for she begs him to send her a few words, poste restante, to Aix-la-Chapelle, letting her know how he is. From this request it seems that she was away from Paris (possibly in or near Poland), but expected to start for the French capital soon and wished to be apprised of his condition at the earliest moment. The anxious tone of the letter leads me to believe that it was written during the last year of the composer's life, when the insidious nature of the disease of which he was a victim had become apparent to himself and his friends. . . . "I cannot," she writes, "wait so long without news of your health and your plans for the future. Do not attempt to write to me yourself, but ask Mme. Etienne, or that excellent grandma, who dreams of chops, to let me know about your strength, your chest, your breathing."

Delphine also was well aware of the unsatisfactory state of his finances, for she writes that she would like to know something about "that Jew; if he called and was able to be of service to you." What follows is in a vein of sadness, showing that her own life was not without its sorrows. "Here everything is sad and lonely, but my life goes on in much the usual way; if only it will continue without further bitter sorrows and trials, I shall be able to support it. For me the world has no more happiness, no more joy. All those to whom I have wished well ever have rewarded me with ingratitude or caused me other _tribulations_." (The _italics_ are hers.) "After all, this existence is nothing but a great discord." Then, with a "_que Dieu vous garde,_" she bids him _au revoir_ till the beginning of October at the latest.

Note that it was in October, 1849, that Chopin took to his deathbed; that in another passage of the letter she advised him to think of Nice for the winter; and that it was from Nice she was summoned to his bedside. It would seem as if she had received alarming advices regarding his health; had hastened to Paris and then to the Riviera to make arrangements for him to pass the winter there; and then, learning that the worst was feared, had hurried back to solace his last hours.

Then came what is perhaps the most touching scene that has been handed down to us from the lives of the great composers. When Delphine entered what was soon to be the death chamber, Chopin's sister Louise and a few of his most intimate friends were gathered there. She took her place by Louise. When the dying man opened his eyes and saw her standing at the foot of his bed, tall, slight, draped in white, resembling a beautiful angel, and mingling her tears with those of his sister, his lips moved, and those nearest him, bending over to catch his words, heard him ask that she would sing.

Mastering her emotion by a strong effort of the will, she sang in a voice of bell-like purity the canticle to the Virgin attributed to Stradella,—sang it so devoutly, so ethereally, that the dying man, "artist and lover of the beautiful to the very last," whispered in ecstasy, "How exquisite! Again, again!"

Once more she sang—this time a

psalm by Marcello. It was the haunted hour of twilight. The dying day draped the scene in its mysterious shadows. Those at the bedside had sunk noiselessly on their knees. Over the mournful accompaniment of sobs floated the voice of Delphine like a melody from heaven.

Chopin died on October 17, 1849, just as the bells of Paris were tolling the hour of three in the morning. He was known to love flowers, and in death he literally was covered with them. The funeral was held from the Madeleine, where Mozart's "Requiem" was sung, the solos being taken by Pauline Viardot-Garcia, Castellan and Lablache. Meyerbeer is said to have conducted, but this has been contradicted. He was, however, one of the pallbearers on the long way from the church to Père la Chaise. When the remains were lowered into the grave, some Polish earth, which Chopin had brought with him from Wola nineteen years before and

THE DEATH OF CHOPIN

From the painting by Barrias

piously guarded, was scattered over the coffin. There is nothing to show what part, save that of a mourner, Delphine Potocka took in his funeral. But though it was the famous Viardot-Garcia whose voice rang out in the Madeleine, it was hers that had sung him to his eternal rest.

How long did Delphine survive Chopin? In 1853 Liszt met her at Baden, postponing his intended departure for Carlsruhe a day in order to dine with her. In May, 1861, he met her at dinner at the Rothschilds'. When Chopin's pupil, Mikuli, was preparing his edition of the composer's works, Delphine furnished him copies of several compositions bearing expression marks and other directions in the hand of Chopin himself. Mikuli dated his edition 1879. It would seem as if the Countess still were living at or about that time.

Besides the aid she thus gave in the preparation of the Mikuli edition of Chopin's works, there is other evidence that she treasured the composer's memory. In 1857, when he had been dead eight years, there was published a biographical dictionary of Polish and Slavonic musicians, a book now very rare. Although the Potocka was only an amateur, her name was included in the publication. Evidently the biographies of living people were furnished by themselves. Chopin's fame at that time did not approximate what it is now. Yet in the second sentence of her biography Delphine records that she was "the intimate friend of the illustrious Chopin."

Forgetting that the line of the Potockis is a long one, the public for years has associated with Chopin the famous pastel portrait of Countess Potocka in the Royal Berlin Gallery. The Countess Potocka of that portrait had a career that reads like a romance, but she was Sophie, not Delphine Potocka. My discovery of a miniature of Countess Sophie Potocka in Philadelphia, painted some fifteen or twenty years later than the Berlin pastel, and of numerous references to her in the diary of an American traveller who was entertained by her in Poland early in the last century, were among the interesting results of my search for information regarding Delphine, but they have no place here. Probably the public, which clings to romance, still will cling to the pastel portrait of Countess Potocka as that of the woman who sang to the dying Chopin—and so the portrait is reproduced here.

Barrias, the French historical painter, who was in Paris when Chopin lived there, painted "The Death of Chopin." It shows Delphine singing to the dying man. As Barrias had his reputation as a historical painter to sustain and as the likenesses of others on the canvas are correct, it is not improbable that he painted Delphine as he saw or remembered her. If so, this is the only known portrait of Chopin's faithful friend, the Countess Delphine Potocka.

Of course no one who undertakes to write about Chopin (or only to read about him for that matter) can escape the episode with Mme. Dudevant,—George Sand,—who used man after man as living "copy," and when she had finished with him cast him aside for some new experience. But the story has been admirably told by Huneker and others and its disagreeable details need not be repeated here. It may have been love, even passion, while it lasted, but it ended in harsh discord; whereas Delphine, sweet and pure and tender, ever was like a strain of Chopin's own exquisite music vibrating in a sympathetic heart.

The Schumanns
Robert and Clara

Robert and Clara

ROBERT and Clara Schumann are names as closely linked in music as those of Robert and Elizabeth Barrett Browning in literature. Robert Schumann was a great composer, Clara Schumann a great pianist. In her dual rôle of wife and virtuosa she was the first to secure proper recognition for her husband's genius. Surviving him many years, she continued the foremost interpreter of his works, winning new laurels not only for herself but also for him. He was in his grave—yet she had but to press the keyboard and he lived in her. Despite the fact that tastes underwent a change and Wagner became the musical giant of the nineteenth century, Clara, faithful to the ideal of her youth and her young womanhood, saw to it that the fame of him whose name

she bore remained undimmed. Hers was, indeed, a consecrated widowhood.

Robert was eighteen years old, Clara only nine, when they first met; but while he had not yet definitely decided on a profession, she, in the very year of their meeting, made her début as a pianist, and thus began a career which lasted until 1896, a period of nearly seventy years! When they first met, Schumann was studying law at the Leipsic University. Born in Zwickau, Saxony, in 1810, he showed both as a boy and as a youth not only strong musical proclivities, but also decided literary predilections. In the latter his father, a bookseller and publisher, who loved his trade, saw a reflection of his own tastes, and they were encouraged rather more sedulously than the boy's musical bent. It was in obedience to his father's wishes that he matriculated at Leipsic, although he composed and played the piano, and his desire to make mu-

ROBERT SCHUMANN

From a portrait by E. Bendemann

sic his profession was beginning to get the upper hand. His meeting with the nine-year-old girl decided him—so early in her life did she begin to influence his career!

Schumann had been invited by his friends, Dr. and Mrs. Carus, to an evening of music, and especially to hear the piano playing of a wonder-child—a "musical fairy," his hostess called her. In the course of the evening he accompanied Frau Carus in some Schubert songs, when, chancing to look up, he saw a child dressed in white, her pretty face framed in dark hair, her expressive eyes raised toward the singer in rapt admiration. The song over, and the applause having died away, he stepped up to the child, laid his hand kindly on her head, and asked, "Are you musical, too, little one?"

A curious smile played around her lips. She was about to answer, when a man came to her and led her to the piano, and the first thing Schumann knew the shapely little hands struck into Beethoven's F-minor Sonata and played it through with a firm, sure touch and fine musical feeling. No wonder she had smiled at his question.

"Was I right in calling her a 'musical fairy'?" asked Frau Carus of Schumann.

"Her face is like that of a guardian angel in a picture that hangs in my mother's room at home," was his reply. Little he knew then that this child was destined to become his own good fairy and "guardian angel." Had he foreseen what she was to be to him, he could not more aptly have described her. The most important immediate result of the meeting was that he became a pupil of her father, Friedrich Wieck, whose remarkable skill as a teacher had carried his daughter so far at such an early age. The lessons stopped when Schumann went to Heidelberg to continue his studies, but he and Wieck, who was convinced of the young man's musical genius, corresponded in a most friendly manner.

Clara, who was born in Leipsic in 1819, became her father's pupil in her fifth year. It is she who chiefly reflected glory upon him as a master, but, among his other pupils, Hans von Bülow became famous, and Clara's half-sister Marie also was a noted pianist. Wieck's system was not a hard-and-fast one, but varied according to the individuality of each pupil. He was to his day what Leschetizky, the teacher of Paderewski, is now. Very soon after her meeting with Schumann, Clara made her public début, and with great success. Among those who heard and praised her highly during this first year of her public career was Paganini.

In 1830, two years after the first meeting of Robert and Clara, Schumann, his father having died, wrote to his mother and his guardian and begged them to allow him to choose a musical career, referring them to Wieck for an opinion as to his musical abilities. The mother wrote to Wieck a letter which is highly creditable to her heart and judgment, and Wieck's reply is equally creditable to him as a friend and teacher. Evidently his powers of penetration led him to entertain the highest hopes for Schumann. Among other things he writes that, with due diligence, Robert should in a few years become one of the greatest pianists of the day. Why Wieck's hopes in this particular were not fulfilled, and why, for this reason, Clara's gifts as a pianist were doubly useful to Schumann, we shall see shortly.

Schumann entered with enthusiasm upon the career of his choice. He left Heidelberg and took lodgings with the Wiecks in Leipsic. Clara, then a mere girl, though already winning fame as a concert pianist, certainly was too young for him to have fallen seriously in love with, or for her to have responded to any such feeling. Even at that early

ROBERT AND CLARA SCHUMANN IN 1847
From a lithograph in possession of the Society of Friends of Music, Vienna

age, however, she exercised a strange power of attraction over him. His former literary tastes had given him a great fund of stories and anecdotes, and he delighted in the evenings to gather about him the children of the family, Clara among them, and entertain them with tales from the Arabian Nights and ghost and fairy stories.

Among his compositions at this time are a set of impromptus on a theme by Clara, and it is significant of his regard for her that later he worked them over, as if he did not consider them in their original shape good enough for her. Then we have from this period a letter which he wrote to the twelve-year-old girl while she was concertizing in Frankfort, and in which the expressions certainly transcend those of a youth for a child, or of an elder brother for a sister, if one cared to picture their relations as such. Indeed, he writes to her that he often thinks of her "not as a brother does of a sister, nor as one friend of another, but as a pilgrim of a distant altar-picture." He asks her if she has composed much, adding, "In my dreams I sometimes hear music—so you must be composing." He confides in her about his own work, tells her that his theoretical studies (with Heinrich Dorn) have progressed as far as the three-part fugue; and that he has a sonata in B minor and a set of "Papillons" ready; then jokingly asks her how the Frankfort apples taste and inquires after the health of the F above the staff in the "jumpy Chopin variation," and informs her that his paper is giving out. "Everything gives out, save the friendship in which I am Fräulein C. W.'s warmest admirer."

For a letter from a man of twenty-one to a girl of twelve, the above is remarkable. If Clara had not afterward become Robert's wife, it would have interest merely as a curiosity. As matters eventuated, it is a charming prelude to the love-symphony of two lives. Moreover,

there seems to have been ample ground
for Schumann's admiration. Dorn has
left a description of Clara as she was
at this time, which shows her to have
been unusually attractive. He speaks
of her as a fascinating girl of thirteen,
"graceful in figure, of blooming complexion, with delicate white hands, a
profusion of black hair, and wise, glow-
ing eyes. Everything about her was ap-
petizing, and I never have blamed my
pupil, young Robert Schumann, that
only three years later he should have
been completely carried away by this
lovely creature, his former fellow-pupil
and future wife." Her purity and her
genius, added to her beauty, may well
have combined to make Robert, musical dreamer and enthusiast on the
threshold of his career, think of her,
when absent, "as a pilgrim of a distant
altar-picture."

She was clever, too, and through her
concert tours was seeing much of the
world for those days. In Weimar she

played for Goethe, the great poet himself getting a cushion for her and placing it on the piano stool in order that she might sit high enough; and not only praising her playing, but also presenting her with his likeness in a medallion. The poet Grillparzer, after hearing her play in Vienna Beethoven's F-minor Sonata, wrote a delightful poem, "Clara Wieck and Beethoven's F-minor Sonata." It tells how a magician, weary of life, locked all his charms in a shrine, threw the key into the sea, and died. In vain men tried to force open the shrine. At last a girl, wandering by the strand and watching their vain efforts, simply dipped her white fingers into the sea and drew forth the key, with which she opened the shrine and released the charms. And now the freed spirits rise and fall at the bidding of their lovely, innocent mistress, who guides them with her white fingers as she plays. The imagery of this tribute to Clara's playing is readily understood. In Paris she heard Chopin and Mendelssohn. All these experiences tended to her early development, and there is little wonder if Schumann saw her older than she really was.

In 1834 Schumann's early literary tastes asserted themselves, but now in connection with music. He founded the "Neue Zeitschrift für Musik," which under his editorship soon became one of the foremost musical periodicals of the day. Among his own writings for it is the enthusiastic essay on one of Chopin's early works, in which Schumann, as he did later in the case of Brahms, discovered the unmistakable marks of genius. The name of Chopin brings me back to Wieck's prophecy regarding Schumann as a pianist. The latter in his enthusiasm devised an apparatus for finger gymnastics which he practised so assiduously that he strained one of his fingers and permanently impaired his technique, making a pianistic career an impossibility. Through this accident he was unable to introduce his own piano works to the public, so that the importance of the service rendered him by Clara, in taking his compositions into her repertoire, both before and after their marriage, was doubled.

One evening at Wieck's, Schumann was anxious to hear some new Chopin works which he had just received. Realizing that his lame finger rendered him incapable of playing, he called out despairingly:

"Who will lend me fingers?"

"I will," said Clara, and sat down and played the pieces for him. She "lent him her fingers;" and that is precisely what she did for him through life in making his piano and chamber music compositions known. Familiarity with Schumann's music enables us of to-day to appreciate its beauty. But for its day it was, like Brahms' music later, of a kind that makes its way slowly. Left to the general musical public, it probably would have been years in sinking into their hearts. Such music requires to be publicly performed by a sympathetic interpreter before receiving its meed of merit. Schumann had hoped to be his own interpreter. He saw that hope vanish, but a lovely being came to his aid. She saw his works come into life; their creation was part of her own existence; she fathomed his genius to its utmost depths; her whole being vibrated in sympathy with his, and when she sat down at the piano and pressed the keys, it was as though he himself were the performer. She was his fingers—fingers at once deft and delicate. She played with a double love—love for him and love for his music. And why should she not love it? She was as much the mother of his music as of his children.

I have already indicated that Clara probably developed early. At all events, there are letters from Schumann to her, at fourteen, which leave no doubt that he was in love with her then, or that she could have failed to perceive this. In one of these letters he proposes this highly poetic, not to say psychological, method of communicating with her. "Promptly at eleven o'clock to-morrow morning," he writes, "I will play the <u>Adagio</u> from the Chopin variations and will think strongly—in fact only of you. Now I beg of you that you will do the same, so that we may meet and see each other in spirit. . . . Should you not do this, and there break to-morrow at that hour a chord, you will know that it is I."

However far the affair may or may not have progressed at this time, there was a curious interruption during the following year. Robert appears to have temporarily lost his heart to a certain Ernestine von Fricken, a young lady of sixteen, who was one of Wieck's pupils. Clara consoled herself by permitting a musician named Banck to pay her attention. For reasons which never have been clearly explained, Schu-

CLARA SCHUMANN AT THE PIANO

mann suddenly broke with Ernestine and turned with renewed ardor to Clara, while Clara at once withdrew her affections from Banck and retransferred them to Schumann. We find him writing to her again in 1835:

"Through all the Autumn festivals there looks out an angel's head that closely resembles a certain Clara who is very well known to me." By the following year, Clara then being seventeen, things evidently had gone so far that, between themselves, they were engaged. "Fate has destined us for each other," he writes to her. "I myself knew that long ago, but I had not the courage to tell you sooner, nor the hope to be understood by you."

Wieck evidently had remained in ignorance of the young people's attachment, for, when on Clara's birthday the following year (1837) Schumann made formal application in writing for her hand, her father gave an evasive answer, and on the suit being pressed, he, who had been almost like a second father to Robert, became his bitter enemy. Clara, however, remained faithful to her lover through the three years of unhappiness which her father's sudden hatred of Robert caused them. In 1839 she was in Paris, and from there she wrote to her father:

"My love for Schumann is, it is true, a passionate love; I do not, however, love him solely out of passion and sentimental enthusiasm, but, furthermore, because I think him one of the best of men, because I believe no other man could love me as purely and nobly as he or so understandingly; and I believe, also, on my part that I can make him wholly happy through allowing him to possess me, and that I understand him as no other woman could."

This love obviously was one not lightly bestowed, but Wieck remained obdurate and refused his consent. Then Schumann took the only step that under the circumstances was possible.

Wieck's refusal of his consent being a legal bar to the marriage, Robert invoked the law to set his future father-in-law's objections aside. The case was tried, decided in Schumann's favor, and on September 12, 1840, Robert Schumann and Clara Wieck were married in the village of Schönefeld, near Leipsic. That year Schumann composed no less than one hundred and thirty-eight songs, among them some of his most beautiful. They were his wedding gift to Clara.

After their marriage his inspiration blossomed under her very eyes. She was the companion of his innermost thoughts and purposes. Meanwhile his musical genius and critical acumen ever were at her command in her work as a pianist. Happily, too, a reconciliation was effected with Wieck, and we find Clara writing to him about the first performance of Schumann's piano quintet (now ranked as one of the finest compositions of its class), on which occasion she, of course, played the piano part.

Four years after their marriage the Schumanns removed to Dresden, remaining there until 1850, when they settled in Düsseldorf, where Robert had been appointed musical director. There was but one shadow over their lives. At times a deep melancholy came over him, and in this Clara discerned with dread possible symptoms of coming mental disorder. Her fears were only too well founded. Early in February, 1854, he arose during the night and demanded light, saying that Schubert had appeared to him and given him a melody which he must write out forthwith. On the 27th of the same month, he quietly left his house, went to the bridge across the Rhine and threw himself into the river. Boatmen prevented his intended suicide. When he was brought home and had changed his wet clothes for dry ones, he sat down to work on a variation as if nothing had

THE SCHUMANN MONUMENT IN THE BONN CEMETERY

happened. Within less than a week he was removed at his own request to a sanatorium at Endenich, where he died July 29, 1856.

Clara survived him forty years, wearing a crown of laurels and thorns — the laurels of a famous pianist, the thorns of her widowhood. It was a widowhood consecrated, as much as her wifehood had been, to her husband's genius. She died at Frankfort, May 19, 1896, and is buried beside her husband in Bonn.

Franz Liszt and His Carolyne

Franz Liszt
and His Carolyne

IN the famous Wagner-Liszt correspondence, Liszt writes from Weimar, under date of April 8, 1853, "Daily the Princess greets me with the lines 'Nicht Gut, noch Geld, noch Göttliche Pracht.'" The lines are from "Götterdämmerung," the whole passage being—

> "Nor goods, nor gold, nor godlike splendor;
> Nor house, nor home, nor lordly state;
> Nor hollow contracts of a treach'rous race,
> Its cruel cant, its custom and decree.
> Blessed, in joy and sorrow,
> Let love alone be."

The lady who according to Liszt daily greeted him with these significant lines was the Princess Carolyne Sayn-Wittgenstein. Since 1848 she and her young daughter Marie had been living with Liszt at the Altenburg in Weimar.

She remained there until 1860, twelve years, when she went to Rome, whither, in due time, Liszt followed her, to make the Eternal City one of his homes for the rest of his life. His last letter to her is dated July 6, 1886, the year and month of his death, so that for a period of nearly forty years he enjoyed the personal and intellectual companionship of this remarkable woman. Their relations form one of the great love romances of the last century.

Liszt's letters to the Princess, written in French and still untranslated, are in four volumes. They were published by the Princess's daughter, Princess Marie Hohenlohe, as a tribute to Liszt the musician and the man. They teem with his musical activities—information regarding the numerous celebrities with whom he was intimate, the musicians he aided, his own great works. But their rarest charm to me lies in the fact that from them the careful reader can glean the whole story of

FRANZ LISZT.
Painting by Ary Scheffer.

the romance of Liszt and Carolyne, from its very beginnings to his death.

We know the fascinating male figure in this romance—the extraordinary combination of unapproached virtuoso, great composer, and man of the world; but who was the equally fascinating woman?

Carolyne von Iwanowska was born near Kiew, Russian Poland, in February, 1819. When she still was young her parents separated, and she divided her time between them. Her mother possessed marked social graces, travelled much, was a favorite at many courts, and, as a pupil of Rossini's in singing, was admired by Spontini and Meyerbeer, and was sought after in the most select salons, including that of Metternich, the Austrian chancellor. From her Carolyne inherited her charm of manner.

Intellectually, however, she was wholly her father's child; and he was her favorite parent. He was a wealthy landed proprietor, and in the administration of his estates, he frequently consulted her. Moreover he had an active, studious mind, and he found in her an interested companion in his pursuits. Often they sat up until late into the night discussing various questions, and both of them — smoking strong cigars!

In 1836 her hand was asked in marriage by Prince Nicolaus von Sayn-Wittgenstein. She thrice refused, but finally accepted him at her father's instigation. The prince was a handsome but otherwise commonplace man, and not at all the husband for this charming, mentally alert and finely strung woman. The one happiness that came to her through this marriage was her daughter Marie.

Liszt came to Kiew on a concert tour in February, 1847. He announced a charity concert, for which he received a contribution of one hundred rubles from Princess Carolyne. He already had heard of her, but she had been described to him as a miserly and peculiar person. The gift surprised him the more for this. He called on her to thank her, found her a brilliant conversationalist, was charmed with her in every way, and concluded that what the gossips considered peculiarities were merely the evidences of an original and positive mentality. Upon the woman, who was in revolt against the restraints of an unhappy married life, Liszt, from whose eyes shone the divine spark, who was as much _au fait_ in the salon as at the piano, and who already had been worshipped by a long succession of women, made a deep impression. Thus they were drawn to each other at this very first meeting.

When, a little later, Liszt took her into his confidence regarding his ambition to devote more time to composition, and communicated to her his idea of composing a symphony on Dante's "Divine Comedy" with scenic illustrations, she offered to pay the twenty thousand thalers which these would cost. Liszt subsequently changed his mind regarding the need of scenery to his "Dante," but the Princess's generous offer increased his admiration for her. It was a tribute to himself as well as to his art, and an expression of her confidence in his genius as a composer (shared at that time by but few) which could not fail to touch him deeply. It at once created a bond of artistic and personal sympathy between them. She was carried away by his playing, and the programme of his first concert which she attended was treasured by her, and after her death, forty years later, was found among her possessions by her daughter.

If it was not love at first sight between these two, it must have been nearly that. Liszt came to Kiew in February, 1847. The same month Carolyne invited him to visit her at one of her country seats, Woronince. Brief correspon-

LISZT AT THE PIANO

dence already had passed between them. To his fifth note he adds, as a post-script, "I am in the best of humor ... and find, now that the world contains Woronince, that the world is good, very good!"

The great pianist continued his tour to Constantinople. When he writes to the Princess from there, he already "is at her feet." Later in the same year he is hers "heart and soul." Early the following year he quotes for her these lines from "Paradise Lost:"

"For contemplation he, and valour formed,
  For softness she, and sweet attractive grace;
  He for God only, she for God in him!"

She presents him with a baton set with jewels; he writes to her about the first concert at which he will use it. He transcribes Schubert's lovely song, "My sweet Repose, My Peace art Thou," and tells her that he can play it only for her. At the same time their letters to each other are filled with references to public affairs and literary, ar-

tistic and musical matters. They are
the letters of two people of broad and
cultivated taste, who are drawn to each
other by every bond of intellect and
sentiment. Is it a wonder that but little more than a year after they met, the
Princess decided to burn her bridges
behind her and leave her husband?
Through his friend, Prince Felix Lichnowsky, Liszt arranged that they
should meet at Krzyzanowitz, one of
the Lichnowsky country seats in Austrian Silesia. "May the angel of the
Lord lead you, my radiant morning
star!" he exclaims. At the same time
he has an eye to the practical side of
the affair, and describes the place as
just the one for their meeting point, because Lichnowsky will be too busy to
remain there, and there will not be a
soul about, save the servants.

It was shortly before the revolution
of 1848. To gain permission to cross
the border, the Princess pretended to
be bound for Carlsbad, for the waters.

Liszt's valet met her and her daughter
as soon as they were out of Russia, took
them to Ratibor, where they were received by Lichnowsky, who conducted
them to Liszt. After a few days at this
place of meeting, they went to Gräz,
where they spent a fortnight in another of the Lichnowsky villas. Among
the miscellaneous correspondence of
Liszt is a letter from Gräz to his friend
Franz von Schober, councillor of lega-
tion at Weimar, where Liszt was settled as court conductor. In it he describes the Princess as "without doubt
an uncommonly and thoroughly brilliant example of soul and mind and intelligence (with a prodigious amount
of _esprit_ as well). You readily will understand," he adds, "that henceforth
I can dream very little of personal ambition and of a future wrapped up in
myself. In political relations serfdom
may have an end; but the dominion of
one soul over another in the spirit re-
gion—should that not remain inde-

structible?"—Oh, Liszt's prophetic soul! Thereafter his life was shaped by this extraordinary woman, for weal and, it must be confessed, for reasons which will appear later, partly for woe.

The Grandduchess of Weimar took the Princess under her protection, and she settled at Weimar in the Altenburg, while Liszt lived in the Hotel zum Erbprinzen. Many tender missives passed between them. "Bonjour, mon bon ange!" writes Liszt. "On vous aime et vous adore du matin au soir et du soir au matin."—"On vous attend et vous bénit, chère douce lumière de mon âme!"—"Je suis triste comme toujours et toutes les fois que je n'entends pas votre voix—que je ne regarde pas vos yeux."

One of the billets relates to an incident that has become historic. Wagner had been obliged, because of his participation in the revolution, to flee from Dresden. He sought refuge with Liszt in Weimar, but, learning that

THE PRINCESS CAROLYNE IN HER LATER YEARS AT ROME

the Saxon authorities were seeking to apprehend him, decided to continue his flight to Switzerland. He was without means and, at the moment, Liszt, too, was out of funds. In this extremity, Liszt despatched a few lines to the Princess. "Can you send me by bearer sixty thalers? Wagner is obliged to flee, and I am unable at present to come to his aid. <u>Bonne et heureuse nuit.</u>" The money was forthcoming, and Wagner owed his safety to the Princess. This is but one instance in which, at Liszt's instigation, she was the good fairy of poor musicians.

About a year after the Princess settled in the Altenburg, Liszt, too, took up his residence there. From that time until they left it, it was the Mecca of musical Europe. Thither came Von Bülow and Rubinstein, then young men; Joachim and Wieniawski; Brahms, on his way to Schumann, who, as the result of this visit from Brahms, wrote the famous article hailing him as the coming

Messiah of music; Berlioz, and many, many others. The Altenburg was the headquarters of the Wagner propaganda. From there came material and artistic comfort to Wagner during the darkest hours of his exile and poverty.

Wendelin Weissheimer, a German orchestral leader, a friend of Liszt and Wagner, and of many other notable musicians of his day, has given in his reminiscences (which should have been translated long ago) a delightful glimpse of life at the Altenburg. He describes a dinner at which Von Bronsart, the composer, and Count Laurencin, the musical writer, were the other guests. At table the Princess did the honors "most graciously," and her "divinity," Franz Liszt, was in "buoyant spirits." After the champagne, the company rose and went upstairs to the smoking-room and music salon, which formed one apartment, "for with Liszt, smoking and music-making were, on such occasions, inseparable." One touch in Weissheimer's description recalls the Princess's early acquired habit of smoking.

"He [Liszt] always had excellent Havanas, of unusual length, ready, and they were passed around with the coffee. The Princess also had come upstairs. When Liszt sat down at one of the two pianos, she drew an armchair close up to it and seated herself expectantly, also with one of the long Havanas in her mouth and pulling delectably at it. We others, too, drew up near Liszt, who had the manuscript of his 'Faust' symphony open before him. Of course he played the whole orchestra; of course the way in which he did it was indescribable; and—of course we all were in the highest state of exaltation. After the glorious 'Gretchen' division of the symphony, the Princess sprang up from the armchair, caught hold of Liszt and kissed him so fervently that we all were deeply moved.

[In the interim her long Havana had gone out.]"

Theyearswhich Liszt passed with the Princess at the Altenburg, and when he was most directly under her influence, were the most glorious in his career. Besides the "Faust" symphony, he composed during this period the twelve symphonic poems, thus originating a new and highly important musical form, which may be said to bear, in their liberation from pedantry, the same relation to the set symphony that the music drama does to opera; the "Rhapsodies Hongroises;" his piano sonata and concertos; the "Graner Messe;" and the beginnings of his "Christus" and "Legend of the Holy Elizabeth." The Princess ordered the household arrangements in such a way that the composer should not be disturbed in his work. No one was admitted to him without her visé; she attended to the voluminous correspondence which, with a man of so much natural courtesy as Liszt, would have occupied an enormous amount of his time. He was the acknowledged head of the Wagner movement, at that time regarded as nothing short of revolutionary; he was looked upon as the friend of all progressive propaganda in his art; to play for Liszt, to have his opinion on performance or composition, was the ambition of every musical celebrity, or would-be one; his coöperation in innumerable concerts and music festivals was sought for. His was a name to conjure with. Between him and these assaults on his almost proverbial kindness stood the Princess, and the list of his great musical productions during this period, to say nothing of his literary work, like the rhapsody on Chopin, is the tale of what the world owes her for her devotion.

The relations between Liszt and the Princess were frankly acknowledged, and by the world as frankly accepted, as if they were two exceptional beings in whom one could pardon things which in the case of ordinary mortals would mean social ostracism. The nearest approach to this situation was that of George Eliot and Lewes. But with Liszt and his Princess the world, possibly after the fashion of the Continent, was far more lenient, and their lives in their outward aspects were far more brilliant. No exalted mind in literature, music, art or science passed through Weimar, or came near it, without being drawn to the Altenburg as by a magnet. There seems to have been within its walls an almost uninterrupted intellectual revel, or, to use a trite expression, which here is most apt, a steady feast of reason and flow of soul. The sojourn of Liszt and the Princess in the Altenburg was a "golden period" for Weimar, a revival of the time when Goethe lived there and reflected his glory upon it.

And yet—convention is the result of the concentrated essence of the expe-

THE ALTENBURG, WEIMAR, WHERE LISZT AND CAROLYNE LIVED

rience of ages; and no one seems able to break through it without the effort leaving a scar. It cast its shadow even over the life at the Altenburg. There remained one great longing to the Princess, the nonfulfilment of which was as a void in her soul. She yearned to bear the name of the man she adored. During the twelve years of their Weimar sojourn she battled for it, but in vain. Then she transferred the battlefield to Rome.

Her husband, a Protestant, had found no difficulty in securing a divorce from her. She was an ardent Roman Catholic, and the church stood in her way, her own relatives, who had been scandalized at her flight, being active in invoking its opposition. She went to Rome in the spring of 1860, to press her suit at the very centre of churchly authority. Liszt remained in Weimar awaiting word from her. It took her more than a year to secure the Papal sanction. Then, when everything seemed auspiciously settled and her marriage with Liszt a certainty, her enthusiasm led her to take a step which, at the very last moment, proved fatal to her long-cherished hope.

Had she returned at once to Weimar, her union with Liszt undoubtedly would have taken place. But no. In her joy she must go too far. In Rome, there where the marriage had been interdicted, there where she had successfully overcome opposition to it, there it should take place. Her triumph should be complete.

Liszt was sent for. His last two letters to her before their meeting in Rome are dated from Marseilles in October, 1861. The marriage was to take place October 22, his fiftieth birthday. He writes her from the Hotel des Empereurs, himself "plus heureux que tous les empereurs du monde!" and again, "Mon long exil va finir." Yet it was only just beginning!

He arrived in Rome on October 20.

All arrangements for the ceremony in the San Carlo al Corso had been made. Then, by a strange fatality, it chanced that several of the Princess's relations, who were most bitter against her, entered upon the scene. Of all times, they happened to be in Rome at this critical moment, and, getting wind of the impending marriage, they entered a violent protest. When, on the evening of the 21st, Liszt was visiting the Princess, a Papal messenger called and announced that His Holiness had decided to forbid the ceremony until he could look into the matter more fully, and requested from her a resubmission of the documents bearing on the case.

To the Princess, then on the threshold of realizing her most cherished hopes, this was the last stroke. Her over-wrought nature saw in it a judgment of Heaven. She refused to resubmit the papers; and even, when a few years later, Prince Wittgenstein died and she was free, she regarded marriage with Liszt as opposed by the Divine will. A strain of mysticism, nurtured by busy ecclesiastics, developed itself in her; she became possessed of the idea that she was a chosen instrument in the Church's hands to further its interests; and with feverish, desperate energy she devoted herself to literary work as its champion. She had her own press, which set up each day's work and showed it to her in proof the next. She did not leave Rome except on one occasion, and then for less than a day, during the remaining twenty-six years of her life.

It has been hinted more than once that the Princess's course was not as completely governed by religious mysticism as might be supposed — that her sensitive nature had divined in Liszt an unexpressed opposition to the marriage, as if, possibly, he did not wish to be tied down to her, yet felt bound in honor, because of the sacrifices she had made for him, to appear to share her hope. La Mara (Marie Lipsius), the editor of the Liszt letters and whose interesting notes form the connecting links in the correspondence, does not take this view. It is noticeable, however, although Liszt and the Princess saw each other frequently whenever he was in Rome, and he became an abbé probably through her influence, that while in some of his letters to her in later years there are notes of regret, those written after the crisis in Rome breathe an intellectual rather than a personal affinity.

Be this as it may, it was a tragedy in his life as well as in her own. Practically the rest of his life was divided, each year, between Budapest, at the Conservatory there; Weimar, but no longer at the Altenburg; and Rome, but not at the Princess's residence, Piazza di Spagna. Thus he had three homes—none of which was home. The "golden period" of his life, as well as the Altenburg itself, where others now were installed, were dim shadows of the past. Liszt was the "grand old man" of the piano, and is a great figure among composers; but whoever knows the story of the last years of his life, sees him a wandering and pathetic figure. He died at Bayreuth in July, 1886; Carolyne survived him less than a year. The literary work of her twenty-six years in Rome probably will be forgotten; it will be the linking of her name with Liszt, and its association with the "golden period" of Weimar, that will cause her to be remembered.

Wagner
and Cosima

Wagner and Cosima

NO woman not a professional musician has ever played so important a part in musical history as "Frau Cosima," the widow of Richard Wagner. In fact, has any woman, professional musician or not? Bear in mind who "Frau Cosima" is. She is the daughter of Franz Liszt, the greatest pianist and one of the great composers of the last century, and was the wife and, in the most exalted meaning of the term, the helpmeet of the greatest of all composers!

The two men with whom Cosima has thus stood in such intimate relation are exceptional even among great musicians. Composers are usually strongly emotional, inspired in all that pertains to their art, but with a specialist's lack of interest in everything else. Not so, however, Liszt or Wagner, for not since the time of Beethoven had there been two musicians who, in the exercise of their art, approached it from so clear an intellectual standpoint. Beethoven through the greatness of his mind was able to enlarge the symphonic form, which had been left by Haydn and Mozart. It became more responsive, more plastic, in his hands. Form in art is the creation of the intellect; what goes into it is the outflow of the heart. Thus Liszt created the Symphonic Poem, and Wagner completely revolutionized the musical stage by creating the Music-Drama. Into the Symphonic Poem, into the Music-Drama, they put their hearts; but the creation of these forms was in each an intellectual _tour de force_. The musician who thinks as well as feels is the one who advances his art. In the historic struggle between Wagner and the classicists Liszt played a large part. He was the first to produce "Lohengrin"—was, as

RICHARD WAGNER

From the original lithograph of the Egusquiza portrait

orchestral conductor, its subtle interpreter, and, thus, a pioneer of the new school; he was Wagner's steadfast champion through life, and a beautiful friendship existed between "Richard" and "Franz."

Even now the reader can begin to realize the rôle Cosima has played in music. That she is the daughter of Liszt is not in itself wonderful, but that she should have fulfilled the mission to which she was born is one of the most exquisite touches of fate. Liszt was one of Wagner's first champions and friends. He came to the composer's aid in the darkest years of his career—during that long exile after Wagner had been obliged to flee from Germany because of his participation in the revolution of 1848. It was, in fact, through Liszt that Wagner received the means to continue his flight from the Saxon authorities and cross the border to safety in Switzerland.

Nor did Liszt's beneficence stop

there. From afar he continued to be Wagner's good fairy. To fully appreciate Liszt's action at this time, one must keep in mind the position of the Saxon composer. To-day his fame is world-wide; we can scarcely realize that there was a time when his genius was not recognized, but at that time he was not famous at all. Those who had the slightest premonition of what the future would accord him were a mere handful of enthusiasts. Such a thing as a Wagner cult was undreamed of. He had produced three works for the stage. "Rienzi" had been a brilliant success, "The Flying Dutchman" a mere succès d'estime, "Tannhäuser" a comparative failure. From a popular point of view he had not sustained the promise of his first work. We know now that compared with his second and third works "Rienzi" is trash, and that rarely has a composer made such wonderful forward strides in his art as did Wagner with "The Flying Dutch-

man" and "Tannhäuser." But that was
not the opinion when they were produced. The former, although it is now
acknowledged to be an exquisitely
poetic treatment of the weird legend,
was voted sombre and dull, and "Tannhäuser" was simply a puzzle. After listening to "Tannhäuser," Schumann
declared that Wagner was unmusical!
Unless a person is familiar with Wagner's life, it is impossible to believe
how bitter was the opposition to his
theories and to his music. Does it seem
possible now that he had to struggle
for twenty-five years before he could
secure the production of his "Ring of
the Nibelung"? Yet such was the case.
Then, too, he was poor, and sometimes
driven to such straits that he contem-
plated suicide.

When the public remained indifferent
to one of his works and critics reviled
it, Wagner's usual method of reply
was to produce something still more
advanced. Thus, when "Tannhäuser"

proved caviar to the public, and seemed to affect the critics like a red rag waved before a bull, he promptly sat down and wrote and composed "Lohengrin." But how should he, an exile, secure its production? There it lay a mute score. As he turned its pages, the notes looked out at him appealingly for a hearing. It was like a homesick child asking for its own. What did Wagner do? He wrote a few lines to Liszt. The answer was not long in coming. Liszt was already making the necessary arrangements to accede to Wagner's request and produce "Lohengrin" in Weimar, where he was musical director. Liszt's name gave great éclat to the undertaking; and through the acclaim which, with the aid of his pupils and admirers, he understood so well how to create, it attracted widespread attention, musicians from far and near in Germany coming to hear it. Of course, opinions on the work were divided, but the band of Wagner enthusiasts received accessions, and the interest in the production had been too intense not to leave an impression. The performance was, in fact, epoch-making. It raised a "Wagner question" which would not down; which kept at least his earlier works before the public; and which made him, even while still a fugitive from Germany, and an exile, a prominent figure in the musical circles of the country that refused him the right to cross its borders.

All this was done by Liszt. Next to Wagner's own genius, which would eventually have fought its way into the open, the influence that first brought Wagner some degree of recognition was Franz Liszt. His assistance to Wagner at this stage in that composer's career cannot be overestimated. He was his tonic in despair, his solace in his darkest hours. Few men appear in a nobler rôle than Liszt in his correspondence with Wagner during this period. Is it not marvellous that some twenty years later, at another crisis in Wagner's life, another being came to his aid and became to him as a haven of rest; and that that being should have been none other than the daughter of his earlier benefactor, Franz Liszt? Fate often is cruel and often unaccountable, but in this instance it seems to have acted the rôle of Cupid with an exquisite sense of what was appropriate, and to have set the crowning glory of a great woman's love upon Wagner's career.

When Liszt was producing "Lohengrin," aiding Wagner pecuniarily, and cheering him in his exile, Cosima Liszt was a young girl in Paris, where she, her elder sister Blandine (afterward the wife of Emile Ollivier, who became the war minister of Napoleon the Third) and her brother Daniel lived with Liszt's mother. It was in Mme. Liszt's house that Wagner first met her. He had gone to Paris in hopes of furthering his cause there. During his sojourn he

COSIMA, WIFE OF WAGNER

From a portrait bust made before her marriage

held a reading of his libretto to "The Ring of the Nibelung" at Mme. Liszt's before a choice audience, which included Liszt, Berlioz and Von Bülow. This occurred in the early fifties. Cosima, who was among the listeners, was at the time fifteen or sixteen years old. The mere fact of her presence at the reading is recorded. Whether she was impressed with the libretto or its author we do not know. It is probable that their meeting consisted of nothing more than the mere formal introduction of the composer to the girl who was the daughter of his friend Liszt, and who was to be one of the small and privileged gathering at the reading. Wagner soon left Paris, and if she made any impression on him at that time, he does not mention the fact in his letters.

Whoever takes the trouble to read Liszt's correspondence, which is in seven volumes and nearly all in French, will have little difficulty in discerning that Cosima was his favorite child. He speaks of her affectionately as "Cosette" and "Cosimette." Like his own, her temperament was artistic and responsive, and she also inherited his charm of manner and his exquisite tact, which, if anything, her early bringing up in Paris enhanced. In 1857, when she was twenty, Wagner saw her again and describes her as "Liszt's wonderful image, but of superior intellect."

Well might Wagner speak of her resemblance to her father as wonderful. I have seen Liszt and Cosima together, on an occasion to be referred to later, and was struck with the remarkable likeness between father and daughter.

Both were idealists; if he had his eyes upon the stars, so had she. Here is a passage from one of Liszt's letters:

"Une pensée favorite de Cosima: 'De quelque coté qu'un tourne la torche, la flamme se redresse et monte vers le ciel.'" ("A favorite thought of Cosima's: 'Whichever way you may turn the torch, the flame turns on itself and still points toward the heavens.'")

A woman whose life holds that motto is in herself an inspiration. Whatever turn fortune takes, her aspirations still blaze the way. She herself is the torch of her motto.

Although not a musician, although keeping herself consistently in the background during Wagner's life (much as a mere private secretary would), her influence at Bayreuth was continually felt; and since his death she has been the head and front of the Wagner movement, and yet without seeking publicity. Her intellectual force quietly assured her the succession. There have been protests against her absolute rule, but she has serenely ignored them. She still moulds to her will all the forces concerned in the Bayreuth productions.

When Mme. Nordica was preparing to sing "Elsa" at Bayreuth, it was Frau Cosima who went over the rôle with her, sometimes repeating a single phrase a hundred times in order to assure the correct pronunciation of one word. It taxed the singer to the utmost; but she found Wagner's widow willing to work as long and as hard as she herself would. The performance established Mme. Nordica as a Wagner singer. Despite the criticisms that have been heaped upon Frau Wagner for assuming to set herself up as the great conservator of Wagnerian traditions, it is significant that when, some years later, Mme. Nordica decided to add "Sieglinde" to her repertoire, but with no special purpose of singing it at Bayreuth, she arranged with Frau Cosima to go over the rôle with her, and in order to do so made a trip to Switzerland, where the former was staying. So far as adding to her reputation was concerned, there was not the slightest reason for Mme. Nordica to do this. That the American prima donna elected to study with Frau Cosima shows that she must have found Wagner's widow a woman of rare temperament.

Cosima was not Wagner's first love, nor even his first wife. For in November, 1836, he had married Wilhelmina Planer, the leading actress of the theatre in Magdeburg where he was musical director of opera. Her father was a spindle-maker. It is said that her desire to earn money for the household, rather than the impetus of a well-defined histrionic gift, led her to go on the stage; but, once on the stage, she discovered that she had unquestionable talent, and played leading characters in tragedy and comedy with success.

Minna is described as handsome, but not strikingly so; of medium height and slim figure, with "soft, gazelle-like eyes which were a faithful index of a tender heart." Later, however, the Princess Sayn-Wittgenstein wrote to Liszt that she was too stout, but praised her management of the household and her excellent cuisine. Her nature was the very opposite of Wagner's. Where he was passionate, strong-willed and ambitious, she was gentle, affectionate and retiring. Where he yearned for conquest, she wanted only a well-regulated home. But she could not follow him in his art theories, and as they assumed more definite shape she became less and less able to comprehend them and, finally, they became almost a sealed book to her.

Doubtless, the ill success of "The Flying Dutchman" and "Tannhäuser," works which, after "Rienzi," puzzled people, engendered her first misunderstanding of Wagner's genius. Some may be surprised that this lack of appreciation did not bring about a separation sooner, instead of after nearly a quarter of a century of married life. But when a man is struggling with poverty, the woman who unobtrusively aids him in bearing it is regarded by him as an angel of light, and the ques-

Richard and Cosima Wagner

tion as to whether she appreciates his genius or not becomes a secondary one in the struggle for existence.

But when at last there is some promise of success, some relief from drudgery, and with it a little leisure for companionship—then, too, there is opportunity for an estimate of intellectual quality. Then it is that the man of genius discovers that the woman who has stood by him through his poverty lacks the graces of mind necessary to his complete happiness, and the self-sacrificing wife who has been his drudge, in order that he might the better meet want, and who has perhaps lost her youth and her looks in his service, is forgotten for some one else. The worst of it is that the world forgets her and all she has done for the great man in her quiet, uncomplaining way. The drudge never finds a page in the "Loves of the Poets." The woman who comes in and reaps where the other has sown, does.

Wagner's friend, Ferdinand Praeger, has much to say of Minna's fine qualities. But he also tells several anecdotes which completely illustrate how absolutely she failed to comprehend Wagner's genius and ambition. Praeger visited them in their "trimly kept Swiss chalet" in Zurich in the summer of 1856. One day when Praeger and Minna were seated at the luncheon table waiting for Wagner, who was scoring the "Nibelung," to come down from his study, she asked: "Now, honestly, is Richard really such a great genius?" Remember that this question was asked about the composer of "The Flying Dutchman," "Tannhäuser" and "Lohengrin." If she was unable to discover his genius in these, how could she be expected to follow its loftier flights in his later works?

On another occasion when Wagner was complaining that the public did not understand him, she said: "Well, Richard, why don't you write something for the gallery?" So little did she understand the man whose genius was founded upon unswerving devotion to artistic truth.

During Praeger's visit, a former singer at the Magdeburg opera and her two daughters called on Wagner. They sang the music of the Rhine-daughters from "Rheingold." When they finished singing, Minna asked Praeger: "Is it really as beautiful as you say? It does not seem so to me, and I'm afraid it would not sound so to others."

While, as can be shown from passages in his correspondence, Wagner appreciated the homely virtues of his first wife, and never, even after they had separated, allowed a word to be spoken against her, the last years of their married life were stormy. She had been tried beyond her strength, and, not sharing her husband's enormous confidence in his artistic powers, she had not the stimulus of his faith in his ultimate success to sustain her. Moreover a heart trouble with which she was afflicted resulted, through the strain to which their uncertain material condition subjected her, in a growing irritability which was accentuated by jealousy of women who entered the growing circle of Wagner's admirers as his genius began to be appreciated.

The crisis came in 1858, when they separated, Minna retiring to Dresden. Two years later, when Wagner was ill in Paris, she went there and nursed him, but they separated again. An interesting fact, not generally known, is that, in 1862, when Wagner was in Biebrich on the Rhine composing his "Meistersinger," Minna came from Dresden as a surprise to pay him a visit—evidently an effort to effect a reconciliation. Wendelin Weissheimer, a conductor at the opera in Mayeuse on the opposite bank of the river and a close friend of Wagner's at that

RICHARD AND COSIMA WAGNER ENTERTAINING IN THEIR HOME WAHNFRIED, LISZT, AND HANS VON WOLZOGEN.

Painting by W. Beckmann.

time, has left an enlightening record of the episode.

Wagner, he says, "the heaven-storming genius, who knew no bounds, tried to play the rôle of Hausvater—of loving husband and comforter. He had some cold edibles brought in from the hotel, made tea, and himself boiled half a dozen eggs. [What a picture! The composer of "Tristan" boiling eggs!] Afterwards he put on one of his familiar velvet dressing-gowns and a fitting barretta, and proceeded to read aloud the book of 'Die Meistersinger.'

"The first act passed off without mishap save for some unnecessary questions from Minna. But at the beginning of the second act, when he had described the stage-setting—'to the right the cobbler shop of Hans Sachs; to the left,' etc.,—Minna exclaimed:

"'And here sits the audience!' at the same time letting a bread-ball roll over Wagner's manuscript. That ended the reading."

The visit of course was futile. Minna returned to Dresden, where she died in 1866. Poor Minna! A good cook, but she did not appreciate his genius, would seem to sum up her story. Yet it is but just that we should pay at least a passing salute to this woman who was the love of Wagner's youth and the drudge of his middle life, and who, from the distance of her lonely separation, saw him basking in the favor of the king, who, too late for her, had become his munificent patron.—What a contrast between her fate and Cosima's!

Were it not for Liszt's letters, meagre would be the information regarding Cosima before her marriage to Wagner. But by going over his voluminous correspondence and picking out references to her here and there, I am able to give at least some idea of her earlier life.

This extraordinary woman, who brought Wagner so much happiness and of whom it may be said that no other woman ever played so important a part in the history of music, came to her many graces and accomplishments by right of birth. She was the daughter of Liszt and the Countess d'Agoult, a French author, better known under her pen name of "Daniel Stern." Thus she had genius on one side of her parentage and distinguished talent on the other; and, on both sides, rare personal charm and tact.

The Countess d'Agoult's father, Viscount Flavigny, was an old Royalist nobleman. While an émigré during the revolution, he had married the beautiful daughter of the Frankfort banker, Bethman. After the Flavignys returned to France, their daughter, an extremely beautiful blonde, was brought up, partly at the Flavigny château, partly at the Sacré Cœur de Marie, in Paris. Talented beyond her years, her wit and beauty won her much admiration. At an early age she married Count Charles d'Agoult, a French officer, a member of the old aristocracy and twenty years her senior.

When she first met Liszt she was twenty-nine years old, had been married six years and was the mother of three children. She still was beautiful, and in her salon she gathered around her men and women of rank, _esprit_ and fame. In 1835 Liszt left Paris after the concert season there. The Countess followed him, and the next heard of them they were in Switzerland. They remained together six years, Cosima, born in 1837, being one of the three children resulting from the union. In the Countess's relations with Liszt there appears to have been a curious mingling of _la grande passion_ and hauteur. For when, soon after she had joined him in Switzerland, he urged her to secure a divorce in order that they might marry, she drew herself up and replied: "Madame la Comtesse d'Agoult ne sera jamais Madame Liszt!" Certainly none but a Frenchwoman would have been capable of such a reply under the same circumstances. Equally French was her husband's remark when, the Countess's support having been assumed by Liszt, he expressed the opinion that throughout the whole affair the pianist had behaved like a man of honor.

After the separation of Liszt and Countess d'Agoult, he entrusted the care of the three children to his mother. During a brief sojourn in Paris, Wagner met Cosima, then a girl of sixteen, for the first time. She formed with Liszt, Von Bülow, Berlioz and a few others the very small, but extremely select, audience which, at the house of Liszt's mother, heard Wagner read selections from his "Nibelung" dramas. In 1855, the burden of the care of the children falling too heavily upon Liszt's mother, the duty of looking after the daughters was cheerfully undertaken by the mother of Hans von Bülow, who resided in Berlin.

In a letter written by Von Bülow in June, 1856, he speaks of them in these interesting terms: "These wonderful girls bear their name with right—full of talent, cleverness and life, they are interesting personalities, such as I have rarely met. Another than I would be happy in their companionship. But their evident superiority annoys me, and the impossibility to appear sufficiently interesting to them prevents my appreciating the pleasure of their society as much as I would like to—there you have a confession, the candor of which you will not deny. It is not very flattering for a young man, but it is absolutely true." Yet, a year later, he married Cosima, one of the girls whose "superiority" so annoyed him.

How strange, in view of what happened later, that Von Bülow so planned his wedding trip that its main objective was a visit to Zurich in order that he might present Cosima to Wagner, who had not seen her since she had formed one of his audience at the "Rheingold" reading in Paris. It is in a letter to his friend, Richard Pohl, written the day before his wedding, that Von Bülow mentions the "Wagnerstadt," Zurich, as the aim of his wedding journey. Was it Fate—or fatality—that led him thither with Cosima? The daughter of Liszt, the bride of Von Bülow, being conducted on her honeymoon to the very lair of the great composer for whom she was, within a few years, to leave her husband! What wonderful musical links destiny wove in the life of this woman who herself was not a musician!

Hans and Cosima arrived at Zurich early in September. "For the last fortnight," writes Von Bülow, under date of September 19, 1857, "I and my wife have been living in Wagner's house, and I do not know anything else that could have afforded me such benefit, such refreshment as being together with this wonderful, unique man, whom one should worship as a god."

On his side Wagner was charmed with the Von Bülows. In one of his letters he speaks of their visit as his most delightful experience of the summer. "They spent three weeks in our little house; I have rarely been so pleasantly and delightfully affected as by their informal visit. In the mornings they had to keep quiet, for I was writing my 'Tristan,' of which I read them an act aloud every week. If you knew Cosima, you would agree with me when I conclude that this young pair is wonderfully well mated. With all their great intelligence and real artistic sympathy, there is something so light and buoyant in the two young people that one was obliged to feel perfectly at home with them."

Wagner allowed them to depart only under promise that they would return next year, which they did, to find a household on the verge of disruption and to be unwilling witnesses to some of the closing scenes of Wagner's first marriage.

During her childhood in Paris Cosima was frail and delicate. Liszt, in one of his letters, confesses that this caused him to regard her with a deeper affection than he bestowed on her elder sister. Later he speaks of her as a rare and beautiful nature of great and spontaneous charm. A friend of Liszt's who saw her at the Altenburg in 1860 writes that she was pale, slender, wan and thin to a degree, and that she crept through the room like a shadow. Liszt was greatly concerned about her, for the year previous her brother Daniel had died of consumption, and he feared she might be stricken with the same malady.

Daniel's death was a sad experience through which they passed together, and which strengthened the ties of tenderness that drew Liszt to his younger daughter. The son died in his father's arms and in her presence. She had nursed him devotedly in his last illness. "Cosima tells me," Liszt wrote, before he had seen Daniel on his sick-bed, "that the color of his beard and of his hair has taken on a touch of brownish red, and that he looks like a Christ by Correggio." Together, after Daniel's death, they knelt beside his bed "praying to God that His will be done—and that He reconcile us to that Divine will, in according us the grace on our part to accept it without a murmur."

Such a scene was a memory for a lifetime. Cosima herself, in one of her letters, gives a beautiful description of her brother's passage from life. "He fell back into the arms of death as into those of a guardian angel, for whom he had been waiting a long time. There was no struggle; without a distaste for life, he seemed, nevertheless, to have aspired ardently toward eternity."

With a pretty touch Liszt gives an idea of Cosima's interest in others. It seems that a certain Frau Stilke was anxious to possess a gray dress of moiré antique, and Liszt had persuaded the Princess Sayn-Wittgenstein to place the necessary sum for buying it at his daughter's disposal. "In order to estimate the cost," he writes, "Cosette has devised this excellent formula: It should be a dress such as one would give to persons who want a dress—only it is necessary that it should be gray and of moiré antique to satisfy the ideal of taste of the person in question."

Wagner does not seem to have seen Cosima after the Von Bülows' second visit to him at Zurich until they came to him for a visit at Biebrich during the summer of 1862. What a contrast Cosima must have seemed to poor Minna who, in the same house and but a short time before, had desecrated the manuscript of "Die Meistersinger" by allowing a bread-ball to roll over it! Wagner's favorable opinion of Hans and Cosima underwent a great change during their sojourn with him. In a letter, after speaking of Von Bülow's depression owing to poor health, he writes: "Add to this a tragic marriage; a young woman of extraordinary, quite unprecedented, endowment, Liszt's wonderful image, but of superior intellect."

That this woman who so impressed Wagner was in her turn filled with admiration for his gifts appears from two letters which, during the summer of 1862, she wrote from Biebrich to her father. In one of these she speaks enthusiastically of some of the "Tristan" music. The other letter concerns "Die Meistersinger:"

"The 'Meistersinger' is to Wagner's other conceptions what the 'Winter's Tale' is to Shakespeare's other works. Its fantasy is founded on gayety and drollery, and it has called up the Nuremberg of the Middle Ages, with its guilds, its poet-artisans, its pedants, its cavaliers, to draw forth the freshest laughter in the midst of the highest, the most ideal poetry."

It is evident that two souls so sympathetic could not long remain in proximity without craving a closer union. "Coming events cast their shadows before," remarks one who often was present during the Biebrich visit of the Von Bülows to Wagner.

How deeply Cosima sympathized with Wagner's aims even then is shown by another episode of this visit. One evening the composer outlined to his friends his plans for "Parsifal," adding that it probably would be his last work. The little circle was deeply affected, and Cosima wept. Strange prescience! "Parsifal" was not produced until twenty years later, yet it proved to be the finale of Wagner's life's labors.

The incident has interest from another point of view. It shows that Wagner had his plans for "Parsifal" fairly matured in 1862, and that it was not, as some critics, who see in it a decadence of his powers, claim, a late afterthought, designed to give to Bayreuth a curiosity somewhat after the <u>façon</u> of the Oberammergau "Passion Play." Decadence? Henry T. Finck, the most consistent and eloquent champion Wagner has had in America, sees in it no falling off in the composer's genius; nor do I. Wagner's scores always fully voice his dramas,—"Parsifal" as completely as any. The subject simply required different musical treatment from the heroic "Ring of the Nibelung" and the impassioned "Tristan."

In a letter written by Wagner in June, 1864, occurs this significant sentence: "There is one good being who brightens my household." The "good being" was Cosima, who from now on was destined to fill his life with the sunshine of love and of devotion to his art.

"Since I last saw you in Munich," Wagner writes to a friend, "I have not

again left my asylum, which in the
meanwhile also has become the refuge
of her who was destined to prove that
I could well be helped, and that the
axiom of my many friends, that 'I could
not be helped,' was false! She knew
that I could be helped, and has helped
me: she has defied every disapproba-
tion and taken upon herself every con-
demnation."

This was written in June, 1870, a year
after Cosima had borne him Siegfried,
and two months before their marriage.
For in August, 1870, the following an-
nouncement was sent out:

"We have the honor to announce our
marriage, which took place on the 25th
of August of this year in the Protestant
Church in Lucerne.

Richard Wagner.
Cosima Wagner, née Liszt.

"August 25, 1870."

When, in 1882, I attended the first performance of "Parsifal" in Bayreuth,

I had frequent opportunity of seeing Wagner and Frau Cosima. Probably the best view I had of them together, and of Franz Liszt at the same time, was at a dinner given by Wagner to the artists who took part in the performances. It was in one of the restaurants near the theatre on the hill overlooking Bayreuth. Wagner's entrance upon the scene was highly theatrical. All the singers and a few other guests had been seated, and Liszt, Frau Cosima and Siegfried Wagner were in their places when the door opened and in shot Wagner. It was as well calculated as the entrance of the star in a play. On his way to his seat he stopped and chatted a few moments with this one and that one. Instead of Wagner sitting at the head of the table and his wife at the foot, they sat together in the middle. It seemed impossible for him, though, to remain seated more than a few minutes at a time, and he was jumping up and down and run-

ning about the table all through the
banquet. On the other side of Wagner
sat Liszt; on the other side of Frau
Cosima, Siegfried Wagner, then still
a boy. Among the four there were two
pairs of likenesses. Liszt was gray;
but, although Frau Cosima's hair was
blonde, and her face smooth and fair as
compared with her father's, which was
furrowed with age and boldly aquiline,
she was his child in every lineament.
Moreover, the quick, responsive light-
ing up of the features, her graceful
bearing, her tact—that these were inherited from him a brief surveillance
of the two sufficed to disclose. Combined with these fascinating, but after
all more or less superficial character-
istics was the stamp of a rare intellectual force on both faces. No one seeing them together needed to be told
that Cosima was a Liszt.

Nor did any one need to be told that
Siegfried was a Wagner. The boy was
as much like his father as his mother

was like hers. Feature for feature, Wagner was reproduced in his son. That there should be no trace of the mother, and such a mother, in the boy's face struck me as remarkable; but there was none. Siegfried Wagner was a veritable pocket edition of his famous father. His later photographs as a young man show that much of this likeness has disappeared. After dinner, there were speeches. Wagner, his hand resting affectionately on Liszt's shoulder, paid a feeling tribute to the man who had befriended him early in his career and who had given him the precious wife at his side. I remember as if it had been but last night the tenderness with which he spoke the words die theure Gattin.

It was a wonderful two or three hours, that banquet, with the numerous notabilities present, and at least two great men, Liszt and Wagner, and one great woman, the daughter of Liszt and the wife of Wagner; and the experience is to be treasured all the more, because few of those present saw Wagner again. Early in the following year he died at Venice. He is buried in the garden back of Wahnfried, his Bayreuth villa. He was a great lover of animals, and at his burial his two favorite dogs, Wotan and Mark, burst through the bushes that surround the grave and joined the mourners. One of these pets is buried near him, and on the slab is the inscription: "Here lies in peace Wahnfried's faithful watcher and friend—the good and handsome Mark."

What Cosima was to Wagner is best told in Liszt's words, written to a friend after a visit to Bayreuth, in 1872, when his favorite child had been married to Wagner two years. "Cosima still is my terrible daughter, as I used to call her, —an extraordinary woman and of the highest merit, far above vulgar judgment, and worthy of the admiring sentiments which she has inspired in all who have known her. She is devoted to Wagner with an all-absorbing enthusiasm, like Senta to the Flying Dutchman—and she will prove his salvation, because he listens to her and follows her with keen perception."

That Bayreuth with Wagner's death did not become a mere tradition, that the Wagner performances still continue there, is due to Frau Cosima. She is Bayreuth. No woman has made such an impression on the music of her time as she. Yet she is not a musician!

THE END